I0155822

The Ultimate Urban Legends

By PINK MINT PUBLICATIONS 2007.

The Ultimate Urban Legends

The Ultimate Urban Legends

The Ultimate Urban Legends

Welcome readers,

This is our third book...

We always wanted to do a book on Urban Legends and strange myths, so here it is!

Some of these amazing stories are true but it is up to you to decide which...

So, get friends round, site down and tell each other these weird stories and watch everyone get scared!

So, read on and look out for other future publications from PINK MINT.

Coming soon...

The little book of... mini series

The Ultimate Urban Legends

The Ultimate Urban Legends

The Ultimate Urban Legends

57 Cents - The True Story

A sobbing little girl stood near a small church from which she had been turn away because it "was too crowed."

"I can't go to Sunday School," she sobbed to the pastor as he walked. Seeing her shabby, unkempt appearance, the pastor guessed the reason and taking her by the hand took her inside and found a place for her in the Sunday school class. The child was so happy that they found room for her, that she went to bed that night thinking of the people who have no place to worship Jesus.

Some two years later, this child lay dead in one of the poor tenement buildings and the parents called for the kindhearted pastor, who had befriended their daughter, to handle the final arrangements. As her poor little body was being moved, a worn and crumpled purse was found which seemed to have been rummaged from some trash dump. Inside was found 57 cents and a note scribbled in childish handwriting which read, "This is to help build the little church bigger so more can go to Sunday School. For two years she had saved for this offering of love.

When the pastor tearfully read that note, he knew instantly what he would do. Carrying this note and the cracked, red pocketbook to the pulpit, he told the story of her unselfish love and devotion. He challenged his deacons to get busy and raise enough money for the larger building.

A newspaper learned of the story and published it. It was read by a Realtor who offered them a parcel of land worth many thousands. When told that the church could not pay so much, he offered it for 57 cents. Church members made large donations. Checks came from far and wide.

Within five years the little girl's gift had increased to $250,000.00--a huge sum for that time (near the turn of the century). Her unselfish love had paid a large dividend.

When you are in the city of Philadelphia, look up Temple Baptist Church, with a seating capacity of 3,300 and Temple

University, where hundreds of students are trained. Have a look, too, at the Good Samaritan Hospital and at a Sunday School building which houses hundreds of Sunday Schoolers, so that no child in the area will ever need to be left outside Additional during Sunday school time.

In one of the rooms of this building may be seen the picture of the sweet face of the little girl whose 57 cents, so sacrificially saved, made such remarkable history. Alongside of it is a portrait of her kind pastor, Dr. Russel H. Conwell, author of the book, "Acres of Diamonds" A true story, which goes to show WHAT GOD, CAN DO WITH 57 cents.

57 Cents - The True Story - *Hattie May Wiat story*

Here is the true story as told by the pastor himself from the pulpit in 1912. A first-hand account of it is in a sermon delivered December 1, 1912 by Russell H. Conwell, pastor of Grace Baptist Church in Philadelphia. Rev. Conwell said the little girl's name was Hattie May Wiatt.

She lived near a church where the Sunday School was very crowded and he told her that one day they would have buildings big enough to allow every one to attend who wanted to. Later, Hattie May Wiatt became sick and died. Rev. Conwell was asked to do the funeral and the girl's mother told him that Hattie May had been saving money to help build a bigger church and gave him the little purse in which she had saved 57 cents. Rev. Conwell had the 57 cents turned into 57 pennies, told the congregation the story of little Hattie May and sold the pennies for a return of about $250. In addition, 54 of the original 57 pennies were returned to Rev. Conwell and he later put them up on display. This was in 1886 when 57 cents was no small savings account for a little girl from a poor family.

Some of the members of the church formed what they called the Wiatt Mite Society which was dedicated to making Hattie May's 57 cents grow as much as possible and to buy the property for the Primary Department of the Sunday school. A house nearby was purchased with the $250 that Hattie May's 57 cents had produced and the rest is history. The first classes of Temple College, later Temple University, were held in that house. It was later sold to allow Temple College to move and the growth of Temple, along with the founding of the Good Samaritan Hospital (Now the Temple University Hospital) have been powerful testimonies to Hattie May Wiatt's dream.

The Charred Scuba Diver

To help put out a forest-fire helicopters sometimes scoop large containers of water out of lakes and oceans to dump on the blazes. During one such occasion a man enjoying a bit of scuba-diving was accidentally scooped up and dropped into the burning trees.

Curses, Broiled Again!

A woman decided at the last minute to get a quick tan for a special occasion. When she found out about the limits the salons set on their tanning beds, she signed up at several different tanning salons. A few days later, her husband told her she "smelled funny". She showered and showered but the smell wouldn't go away. When she finally went to the doctor he ran some tests and told her: "I'm sorry, it seems you've microwaved your internal organs, there's nothing we can do for you."

The Fatal Boot

Over a hundred years ago, a cowboy shot a rattlesnake. It wasn't dead, so he stomped it to death. Within a few days, the man took ill and died mysteriously. When his son was grown, he proudly took his fathers favourite boots as his own, a few days later he turned grey and died. His wife had been pregnant at the time, and when her son was grown she gave him the boots, telling him "You're father and your grandfather died in these boots, take good care of them." A few days later he died. Finally someone noticed that in the heel of the boot was the rattlesnake's fang and it had enough venom left for several more generations.

Noodles!

A man was cooking Oodles of Noodles and accidentally spilled the pan of boiling water and noodles onto his bare feet. The heat causing his pores to open and the noodles to enter his skin.

The Pig on the Road

A state trooper was driving through a rural area one day and as he passed by a farm, the farmer yelled "PIG! PIG!" at him while shaking a pitchfork. The trooper wasn't the sensitive type and began yelling out the window "Redneck! Redneck!" as he ran into the large pig crossing the road.

The Titanic

The construction of the ship was at such a fast pace that at least one worker was accidentally walled up in hull and left to die.

Catholic workers in Belfast almost stopped construction on the ship because the hull number 3909 04 seemed to spell out "NO POPE" when viewed in a mirror.

A cursed mummy that had already caused several deaths was in the cargo hold when the ship sunk.

The Titanic was the first ship to use SOS as a distress call.

Black Aggie

There is a legend about Druid Ridge Cemetery in Baltimore, Maryland. It is locally well-known for it being the former home of a statue known as Black Aggie. In the early part of the century, there was a woman named Aggie, who was a nurse working at a hospital. She was congenial and well-liked, but it seemed that patients under her care always seemed to die. Superstition grew, and she was put to death, which turned out to be a mistake when she was discovered innocent the very next day. A communal feeling of guilt spread, so a statue was put in Druid Ridge Cemetery in her honour. This became the second mistake, when strange occurrences started happening.

Legend has it that if you stand before it at the stroke of midnight, you will be struck blind by the statue's red glowing eyes. People were even found dead in front of it, including a pledge from a local fraternity. Another rumour is that pregnant women who walked in the figure's shadow (where oddly, the grass never grew) would suffer miscarriages. People would gather at the graveyard at night, which became a frequent problem.

All of this finally came to a climax one morning when the cemetery employees walked into work only to find Black Aggie with one of her arms sawed off. Upon investigating this, the arm of the statue and a saw were found in the backseat of a worker's car. The man was brought to trial, and he claimed Black Aggie cut off one of her arms and had given it to him in a fit of grief. Some people believed the ironic story, but it wasn't enough for the court. He was found guilty.

Eventually the statue was removed from Druid Ridge Cemetery, and was donated to a Baltimore museum. It was never displayed however, and resided in the basement. Occasionally, people still congregate at the cemetery in pursuit of truth in the legend, but it is no longer the location of fraternity stunts.....

Alligators in the Sewer

It used to be a trend for parents returning home from Florida vacations to bring back small, baby alligators for their to raise as , particularly in New York. Once the babies grew up, they were no longer cute or convenient. So, to get rid of them New Yorkers resorted to flushing the little guys down the toilet.

Some of these washed up gators survived in the city's sewer system and began to breed. Now there are full-grown alligators living under the streets of Manhattan. It's been said that the animals are blind and albino, having lost their eyesight and the pigment in their hides because they live in constant darkness.

The alligators grew to monstrous sizes and are "mutants."

The Ultimate Urban Legends

The Amityville Horror

Everybody in Amityville knows about the house on Ocean Ave. Was it real or a hoax? Most people seem to think that it was just a hoax, but most famous paranormal investigators still maintain the house is haunted by an evil presence.

Amityville House

In November 1974, Ronald DeFeo murdered his entire family, shooting them all with a .35 Marlin Rifle. According to DeFeo he was being controlled by evil spirits and heard voices. He was sentenced to six life sentences. A year later Kathy and George Lutz moved in. They moved out after a month. They made incredible claims of black ooze coming from toilets, doors blown off hinges, unexplained teeth marks, a pit to hell in the basement, and of course the bleeding walls. It was a little too sensational for most people to believe. But there were some remarkable things that did have some truth. George Lutz did look very much like Ronald DeFeo. So much it is literally scary. The stories that the Lutz's told sounded like previous cases of demonic possession, but many claimed they were just rumours.

The stories spawned numerous books, movies, and a cult following. There are stories about the property being built on Indian Burial grounds, an Indian sanatorium, or even a supposed witch living on the property from Salem Massachusetts. None of the claims have been proven.

Recently the house has been occupied by new owners, they have reported nothing unusual.

Another Hookman

On a summer night in Pennsylvania, a boy and a girl drive out to a spot in the woods. Parked in the darkness, they heard on the radio that a man escaped from Allentown State Hospital, several miles from the local high school, and was terrorizing innocent people on a murder-spree. He was described to have lost his hand and years ago it had been replaced by a large metal hook. He had hacked off his own hand in a fit of madness, trying to escape a pair of handcuffs years earlier.

The boy thought nothing of it, switched off the radio and turned his attention to his girlfriend.

Suddenly, small noises erupted from nearby. The girl pulled away, frightened. "I'm scared. You know, about what they said on the radio? Maybe we should go home."

"No way, do you want your parents to find out we didn't go to the movies? Just relax." As they picked up where they left, they didn't hear anything for a while until there was a loud screech on the door, obviously coming from the girl's side of the car.

"That's it, take me home! It's not safe out here!"

Her boyfriend, senselessly frustrated, reluctantly agreed. He complained all the way home, insulting her for "being such a baby". Barely waiting for the car to stop, the girl angrily opened the door and got out of the car as they pulled up to her driveway. Slamming the car door, ready to go inside, she froze, staring at the car. She started to scream.

The boy, growing a bit alarmed, got out of the car and walked around to her side, where he too, stopped where he stood and could only stare at the door handle in frightened amazement. Found hanging from the car door, was a bloody hook, just dangling in place.

Booby-Trapped Toilets

A zero-population-growth terrorism group called "No More" has been setting up little guillotines under the rims of public toilet seats. When a pressure sensor senses someone sitting on the toilet a razor-sharp blade slashes across the front half of the toilet with the purpose of damaging/removing the victim's testicles.

Cheap Terrorist

The Ultimate Urban Legends

A terrorist didn't pay enough postage on a letter bomb. It came back with "return to sender" stamped on it. Confused as to what it was, he opened it and was blown to bits.

Halloween Poisonings

Every Halloween people die from eating candy poisoned by sadistic "teeters". -Although razor blades and needles hidden in apples are relatively common.

9-11

There were no taxis around the World Trade Center at the time of the attack.

Terrorism

The next terrorist attacks will stem from 7-11 stores on the date 7/11.

Theatre Seats

Several people have been stuck with AIDS-infected needles while sitting in movie theatre seats. Sometimes the trapped seats have a note on them welcoming the person to the world of AIDS.

Waterslide Traps

Many have been seriously injured by razor blades stuck to the walls of waterslides with bubble gum.

Y2K Hate Crimes

The FBI has released a report that starting in the beginning of the year 2000 several white-supremist groups plan to shoot minorities on sight.

The Baby in the Chair

A young couple were waiting impatiently to leave on their first vacation since the baby was born but the woman's aunt, who would be babysitting was thirty minutes late. The young woman called her elderly aunt to find out what was going on, and the old woman apologized for her forgetfulness, and said she'd speed right over. Since the aunt was only a couple miles away, the couple decided they'd go ahead and go rather than wait for her and risk missing their flight. Two weeks later when the couple returned they were horrified to find the baby still in it's high-chair where they'd left it, except now it was dead and bloated, and covered with flies. The aunt really had sped, and unfortunately crashed and died before she made it over.

The Baby on the Roof

A young couple were driving down the highway one day and decided it was time to switch drivers. As they changed places they left their infant child on the roof of the car and drove off.

The Babysitting Hippie

A young couple had to resort to a new babysitter one night because their regular sitter was ill. The girl came highly recommended, but the couple were a little put off when she arrived and they discovered she was a hippie. Being a young and open minded couple, they decided to go ahead on to the theatre, but would call and check on the baby and the sitter during intermission. When they called the sitter told the woman everything was "groovy" and she'd even stuffed and roasted the turkey for a nice dinner. The woman told her husband and it occurred to her that she didn't think they'd had a turkey. When they got home, they were shocked to find the babysitter lying on the floor staring blankly into space, obviously on acid or some type of drug. They panicked and looked all over for the baby, but it was nowhere to be found until they came upon it in the kitchen, roasted and partially eaten, wrapped in foil.

The Beheaded Schoolgirl

A young girl was hanging her head out of the school bus window and a road sign lopped it off.

The Can of Worms

Two guys saw a kid fishing at a lake one day. One of them asked if the fish were biting and the kid replied with an annoyed look on his face: "No, but the worms are!" Surprised and amused, the men laughed and went on.

On the way back they were even more surprised when they saw the boy was slumped over his fishing pole dead, his "can of worms" was filled with baby water moccasins.

The Disguised Child

A small child was abducted away from her parents at Disneyworld. The distraught parents are taken to a surveillance room filled with monitors to look for the child. Almost at the point of giving up, the mother recognizes the child's shoes when a strange woman attempts to leave the park. The reason the shoes were all that were recognized is the child's hair had been cut and died, and she'd been dressed as a little boy.

-No child has ever been abducted at Disneyworld or Disneyland. Sometimes this one takes place in other amusement parks. or even supermarkets.

God Took Them

When a little girl's cat had kittens they disappeared after a couple of days, when she asked her mother what happened to them and her mother said "God took them." Months later the cat again had a litter of kittens. Her mother sent her out to run some errands, but before she left she wanted to play with the kittens again. She heard her father coming carrying a bucket and hid from him. She watched while her father put the kittens in a sack and drowned them in the bucket. Later the girl again asked her mother what happened to the kittens. Her mother said "God took them." Several days later the mother asked the girl to watch her brother in the bath tub while she answered the phone. The mother screamed when she came into the bathroom after a few minutes. The girl told her "God took him."

-Serves 'em right. Anyone too stupid to take care of responsibly shouldn't breed

Mommy's Little Helper

A young girl watched her mother scold her younger brother for again wetting his pants by yelling that the next time it happened she was going to 'cut it off!" A few days later the mother returned from shopping to find her daughter waiting at the door with a bloody kitchen knife, she said "Timmy wet his pants, but don't worry it won't happen again 'cause I did just like you said."

Babysitting is a Dangerous Job

A young couple went out to dinner one evening and left the baby-sitter in charge of their two. They had been put to bed and the baby-sitter was watching the television when the phone rang. She answered but all she heard was a man laughing hysterically and then a voice saying, "I'm upstairs with the children, you'd better come up." Thinking it was "one of those prank phone calls" or a practical joke she slammed down the receiver and turned the television sound up.

A short time later the phone rang again and, as she picked it up, the unmistakable hysterical laughter came down the line and the voice once again said "I'm upstairs with the children, you'd better come up." Getting rather frightened she called the operator and was advised they would notify the police and, should he phone again, could she keep him talking in order to give them time to trace the call and have him arrested.

Minutes after she replaced the receiver the phone rang again and, when the voice said, "I'm upstairs with the children, you'd better come up," she tried to keep him talking. However, he must have guessed what she was trying to do and he put the phone down.

Only seconds later the phone rang again, this time it was the operator who said, "Get out of the house straight away, the man is on the extension". The baby- sitter put down the phone and just then heard someone coming down the stairs. She fled from the house and ran straight into the arms of the police. They burst into the house and found a man brandishing a large butcher's knife. He had entered the house through an upstairs window, murdered both the children and was just about to do the same to the poor baby-sitter.

Check the Back Seat!

A friend stopped at a pay-at-the- pump gas station to get gas. Once she filled her gas tank and after paying at the pump and starting to leave, the voice of the attendant inside came over the speaker. He told her that something happened with her card and that she needed to come inside to pay. The lady was confused because the transaction showed complete and approved. She relayed that to him and was getting ready to leave but the attendant, once again, urged her to come in to pay or there'd be trouble. She proceeded to go inside and started arguing with the attendant about his threat. He told her to calm down and listen carefully: He said that while she was pumping gas, a guy slipped into the back seat of her car on the other side and the attendant had already called the police. She became frightened and looked out in time to see her car door open and the guy slip out.

Check the Back Seat! Version 2

A woman was driving on her way home when she noticed a big 18 wheeler truck driving behind her. The truck driver flashed his lights at her. She ignored him, but he continued to flash his lights, distracting her from the road. She decided to drive faster to try to move away from the annoying truck. The driver caught up with her car and flashed his headlights at her again. She called the police on her cell phone and told them what was happening to her. They instructed her to meet them at her house. When she got there she quickly ran out of the car and up to the police officers waiting for her.

Amazingly, the truck stopped in front of her house as well, despite the police obviously waiting for him. The officers began to arrest the driver, but he begged them to let him explain. He said that when they were stopped at a rest stop at the same time he saw a man get into the back seat of her car with a huge knife. With no other way to warn her about the man, the driver followed the woman and flashed his lights each time he noticed the man rising up out of the back seat to attack her. The killer ducked back down to avoid being seen.

The police searched the car and arrested the would-be killer instantly.

Check the Back Seat! Version 3

One night a woman went out for drinks with her girlfriends and at the end of the night she left the bar alone. On her way home, her route took her onto a deserted highway. She noticed a lone pair of headlights quickly approaching her car from behind. As the car came closer she noticed that its turn signal was on, the car was going to pass.

Just as it moved over to begin passing, suddenly the driver swerved back behind her car, pulled up dangerously close to her tailgate and flashed the high beams at her.

She started getting nervous and kept an eye on the strange vehicle in the rear view mirror. The headlights dimmed for a moment and then the high beams flashed again and the car behind her surged forward. The frightened woman struggled to keep her eyes on the road and fought the urge to keep looking at the car behind her. Finally, she approached her exit but the car continued to follow, flashing the high beams periodically.

Through every stoplight and turn, it followed her until she pulled into her driveway. She figured her only hope was to make a mad dash into the house and call the police. As she flew from the car, so did the driver of the car behind her — and he screamed, "Lock the door and call the police! Call 911!"

When the police arrived the horrible truth was finally revealed to the woman. The man in the car had been trying to save her. As he pulled up behind her and his headlights illuminated her car, he saw the silhouette of a man with a butcher knife rising up from the back seat to stab her, so he flashed his high beams and the figure crouched back down.

The moral of the story: Check the back seat!

Check the Back Seat! Version 4

When she gets to her house she gets out of the car, runs inside and calls the police. She looks out the window and sees the man get out of the vehicle that followed her with a gun in his hand just as the police arrive. The man protests, "Your arresting the wrong guy, I saw a man get into the back seat of her car with a knife and was going to call the police but didn't want to let her out of my sight." Sure enough, when the police looked in the back seat of her car, they found a man with a knife.

Check the Back Seat! Version 5

A girl was traveling to visit a friend and stopped to get gas. When she attempted to return to her car the gas station attendant who had a strong stutter told her to follow him inside as there was a problem with her credit card.

She was suspicious as to why there would be a problem with her card but obliged and went inside. As soon as she walked in, the attendant shut the door behind them and locked it.

The girl started screaming and shouting at him to move out the way. The attendant tried to explain, but his stutter made him difficult to understand. "Th-th- there uh mmm i-i-i-its b-because" The woman was too scared and too impatient to listen to the attendant. She managed to push him aside and get out of the station, but the attendant was running after her.

She rushed back to her car and got in, slammed the door shut and drove off as the attendant was still trying to get his words out "TH-TH-THERE'S SOMEONE IN THE BACK SEAT!!"

The girl wasn't listening, but someone rose up behind her in the back seat with an axe and...

Check the Back Seat! Version 6

A young woman is sitting in a coffee house, about ready to leave, when a man approaches her and asks to buy her a cup of coffee. She politely refuses his offer, and tells the man that she's had enough cups already, and that she's going to leave. She walks out to her car, and drives away. Following her is the man who was refused on his coffee offer in his truck. She drives along a two- lane stretch of road, and sees the man following her in his truck flashing his lights and honking his horn. The woman is under the assumption that he is angered for her refusal of his offer.

After being followed for around 10 minutes with the man following her still flashing the lights and honking, the woman's car runs out of gas. The man pulls behind her on the side of the road and gets out of the car with a double-barrel shotgun.

He tells her to get out of the car. She doesn't at first, then he screams at her "GET OUT OF THE CAR LADY", and she complies.

He then says "Get out of the car." again. She tells him she's already out.

He says "Not you, him". He gestures to the vehicle and she sees a man wielding a butcher's knife get out of the back of the car, holding his knife up in a surrendering style. The man tells the woman that he was flashing his lights and honking his horn so the man with the knife wouldn't harm her.

Was That the Best Man?

A bride and a groom are at their wedding reception. Everything is going perfectly when the groom stands up to give a toast. He thanks all the guests for coming and for the stack of presents on the table. He thanks the father of the bride for the beautiful reception.

He then tells the guests that he has a surprise for all of them. He instructs them to look under their chairs. They do and find a picture taped to the bottom of each seat. The guests are shocked and horrified! It's a picture of the bride and the best man having sex! The groom says he had a feeling they were having an affair and hired an investigator who took the photo. He then says to the father of the bride, "Thanks for the $30,000 sit-down dinner and party, but I'm out of here." And he walked out. He filed for an annulment the following Monday.

Big Liz

Big Liz was a slave girl who lived during the Civil war. Her master used her and his other slaves to deliver supplies to Southern troops. Big Liz managed to tell Union soldiers where the shipments were going, and many deliveries were intercepted by the north.

Her master found out about her deception and plotted to murder the girl. He had a great deal of money and didn't want it to be stolen by the Yankees if his area was taken over, so he commanded Big Liz to help him take the money into a nearby swamp to bury it. As Big Liz was smoothing over the dirt, her master struck her with his knife, cutting her head off. He left her there to die and returned to his plantation without any other living seal knowing the location of his fortune. He was killed sometime during the war and no one ever reclaimed the money that Big Liz buried.

If you want to get the gold for yourself, here is what you need to do.

Over the Transquaking River there is a small white bridge. Park on the bridge, turn off your car and honk your horn three times. Wait. Don't get scared and try to start your car, it won't work. Big Liz will appear holding her head in her hands. If you follow her she will lead you through the trees and mud to where the wealth is hidden, but you won't have the nerve to stay with her and dig up the gold.

Bloody Mary

Now if you follow these instructions, you may be able to see Mary for yourself. At midnight on Friday the 13th, turn off all the lights in your house. Go to the bathroom and turn on the water in the shower and the sink. Flush the toilet, look into the mirror and say "Bloody Mary" 5 times. She will appear in mirror. You need to hurry and turn on the light or she will stab you in the back.

Blow-dried Bunny

A man walked into his garden one day to find his dog with a piece of dirty fur in its mouth. Examination proved that the dirty piece of fur was actualy a prize rabbit belonging to the neighbour. It was very dead, although no obvious injury could be seen.

The man was horrified and felt terrible. He took the rabbit inside, shampooed and blow dried it, then quickly snuck next door to put it back in the hutch before the neighbour got home. A few days went by and he heard nothing. Then on the weekend he was talking over the fence to his neighbour, who he said that a strange thing had happened to him that week. When he came home from work one night he found his prize rabbit dead in its hutch. "Oh, no," says the man. "How awful!"

"That's not the strange part," says the neighbour. "What's weird is that it had died earlier that morning and I buried it before going to work!"

Blue Baby

Go into a bathroom with the lights off and the door closed. Pretend to rock a baby. Chant the phrase "Blue Baby" thirteen times. A baby will appear and scratch you. DROP IT AND RUN! If you don't, a woman will appear and scream as loud as glass breaking, "GIVE ME BACK MY BABY!!!" If you have her baby, she will kill you.

Bonsai Cats

A Japanese man in New York breeds and sells kittens that are called BONSAI CATS.

The Ultimate Urban Legends

That would sound cute, if it weren't kittens that were put in to little bottles after being given a muscle relaxant and then locked up for the rest of their lives! The cats are fed through a straw and have a small tube for their faces. The skeleton of the cat will take on the form of the bottle as the kitten grows. The cats never get the opportunity to move. They are used as original and exclusive souvenirs.

These are the latest trends in New York, China, Indonesia and New Zealand. If you think you can handle it, viewww.bonsaikitten.com and have a look at the methods being used to put these little kittens into bottles. This petition needs 800 names, so please put yours on it! Copy the text into a new email and put your name on the bottom, then send it to everyone you know!

Bride and Seek

During the wedding reception of a young couple, the guests decided to play a drunken game of hide and seek. It was decided that the groom was "it" and he eventually found everyone except his new bride.

The longer he searched the more frustrated he became and he was soon furious thinking she had left. He decided the game wasn't funny anymore and went home without his bride. As weeks went by, he accepted that she'd had second thoughts and went on with her life so he did the same.

A few years later a cleaning lady dusted off an old trunk in the attic of the building where the reception had taken place, out of curiosity she opened it.

Inside the trunk was the rotted body of the missing bride who'd apparently Military became locked in the trunk she'd chosen to hide in. Whether she'd suffocated or starved was unknown, but her face was frozen in a scream.

Buggy Barber

A man living in Kansas hated going to the barber. Thus, he never cut his hair. For 30 years his red hair grew and grew, until it finally reached his ankles. His wife begged him to cut his hair, for people smirked and stared whenever they saw him. He finally agreed, since his hair was annoying and got in his way.

When he arrived at the barber shop, he sat down nervously and waited for his haircut to begin. Half-way through the cut, he jumped up, screaming, and ran out of the shop.

His wife found him dead hours later on their door step, a huge nest of red- backed spiders crawling out of his tangled locks. When the barber was cutting his hair, he upset a nest of poisonous spiders living in the man's hair that bit him to death.

Buggy Burrito

Sara was driving home from work one day and she was starving. Not wanting to worry about cooking dinner once she got home, she decided to stop for some take out. She pulled into her local Taco Bell and ordered a burrito. She enjoyed her quick meal and when she was done she headed home.

When she woke up the next day, her tongue felt sore and a little swollen. It bothered her all day, so she went to see her doctor to find out what was wrong. The doctor didn't find anything on his initial examination, so he told her to come back if it got any worse. Days later her tongue swelled up considerably and became very sore. She went back to the doctor and he decided to do a minor surgery. When the doctor had Military cut open her tongue he found a cyst among her taste buds filled with cockroach eggs. They traced the eggs back to the burrito from her fast dinner.

Car Jacker Warnings

You have just gotten into your automobile and started it when you notice a piece of paper has suddenly appeared on your back window. You immediately get out of your still running automobile to investigate the source of the note when a carjacker appears on the other side, jumps into your car and drives off. The criminal has your car and everything in it including your purse which contains your personal information. : Maggie Smith from Columbia, TN

An attractive professional looking man approaches a lone female in a shopping mall parking lot and asks her to evaluate a new perfume by sniffing a sample sprayed on a handkerchief. Upon sniffing the supposed sample, the unsuspecting woman faints and is abducted by the man. The perfume is actually ether.

Don't trust old people!

A woman is loading her groceries into her car after going shopping at a local supermarket. A strange old lady wearing a dark pair of sunglasses and a big bag approaches her car and asks her for a ride to the bus stop because she had been walking all day and was too tired to walk there.

The lady agrees to drive her and as she finishes loading up her groceries she realizes the old lady keeps staring at her intently. When she gets back into her car she becomes suspicious and pretends that she left her credit card in the store and leaves to go check.

The lady finds a squad car and tells the officer about the strange old woman. When they go back to her car they find her car door wide open, but the old lady is gone. She had left her bag, and when they look inside they find a wig, a dress, a pair of sunglasses, and a big butcher's knife. ,

Spider Eggs Make It Chewy

Bubble Yum was the first soft bubble gum to hit the market, making its debut in 1976. It was an instant success and sales of the candy quickly soared.

Prior to Bubble Yum, bubble gum was hard and took a fair bit of vigorous mastication to render it into a suitably soft bubble-blowing state. Bubble Yum was a breakthrough, a gum that was ready for bubble blowing after being chomped only a few times. As to how soft it was, even a little tyke could squish a block of Bubble Yum between his fingers.

The Ultimate Urban Legends

Any confection that revolutionary is going to spawn speculation among the younger set. "Why is it so chewy?" was the question on everyone's lips. It didn't take long for kids to invent a plausible answer. There had to be something chewy in there. What's more chewy than spider eggs? By the spring of 1977, sales had slipped noticeably. Rumours that Bubble Yum contained spider's eggs or was made from their webs abounded.

Chicken Gun

NASA scientists have commandeered a chicken gun - a device normally used in aircraft safety testing to fire chicken carcasses into airplane windshields at flight speed, approximating the damage caused by bird strikes - to simulate the impact of loose tank foam hitting vulnerable parts of the space shuttle.

Urban legend has it that a group of foreign aerospace engineers once tried to use the American-made chicken gun in their own safety tests, with disastrous results — unaccountably, the poultrified projectile shattered every windshield sample it was fired at, no matter how thick. U.S. experts brought in to solve the problem did so by passing along four simple words of advice: "Thaw the chicken first."

Choking Doberman

A woman returned from work and found her large dog, a Doberman, lying on the floor gasping for air. Concerned over the animal's welfare, she immediately loaded the pet into her car and drove him to a veterinarian.

The vet examined the dog but finding no reason for his breathing difficulties, announced that he'd have to perform a tracheotomy and insert tubes down the animal's throat so he could breathe. He explained that it wasn't anything she'd want to watch and urged the woman to go home and leave the Doberman there overnight.

Ruff! When the woman returned home, the phone was ringing off the hook. She answered it, and was surprised to discover it was the vet. Even more surprising was his message -- "Get out of the house immediately! Go to the neighbour's and Military call the police!" It seems that when the vet performed the operation, he found a very grisly reason for the dog's breathing difficulty -- three human fingers were lodged in its throat. Concerned that the person belonging to the dismembered fingers might still be in the house, he phoned to warn the woman.

According to the story, police arrived at her house and found an unconscious intruder, sans fingers, lying in a closet.

Clown Statue

This girl was babysitting for some family friends one night, a little boy and a little girl. The parents had a fetish for clowns and had collected clowns from around the world for years, setting aside a room in the house just to put them on display. That night, they were playing in this very room. Many of the clowns were just statues, and some were life-size, one in particular, was seated in a small child-like rocking chair.

The babysitter started to feel more and more uneasy about this statue Military throughout the night. She felt as though the eyes were following her, whenever she moved around the room with the. She decided to call the parents. "I'm so sorry to bother you", she said, "but I was wondering if I could move this clown that you have in the rocking chair, it's starting to scare the kids and I." "What clown are you referring to? I don't recall us having a clown fitting that description. Are you sure its sitting in the rocking chair?" the mother asked hurriedly.

"Yes, I'm sure." said the girl. "It's sitting right here, I'm looking at it right now...Why? I know it's probably very old and I shouldn't attempt to move it out of the way."

"Take the kids and get out of the house, now. The neighbour across the street will let you in. Call me immediately when you get there." and with that, the mother hung up. Frightened and confused, the babysitter grabbed the kids and ran out. When she and the kids arrived safely at the neighbours, she called and the mother answered. "What's wrong? Did something happen? Are you all okay?" the girl asked. "Yes, we are fine, but it's not us we are worried about, it's you and the kids. I'm so glad you called--we were afraid this would happen again. We will be there shortly along with the police, I'll explain everything when we get there", and the mother hung up.

The parents later explained to the girl that for some time, the next-door neighbour had been giving them problems. He was mentally ill, heard voices, the whole bit. On numerous occasions he had snuck into their house and tried to kidnap the. This time, he dressed up in a clown suit, painted his face, and waited quietly until he had the opportunity to do what he came to do. The parents had informed the police many times but never had any proof until now about what was happening. They thanked the girl, paid her, and drove her home.

The clown is sometimes in the living room. The clown statue turns out to be a "little person" that was living in the garage for 4 months and would go in and get whenever the parents left the house. This time, he saw the parents leave, and went in to get like he always did, not expecting there to be a babysitter in the living room. Sometimes the babysitter calls the parents asking them if she can put a blanket over the clown statue.

Coat Shopper

A woman went to a coat discount store to buy a new winter coat. She browsed through the latest styles and found a coat that she thought might look nice. She took it off the hanger and tried it on. She enjoyed the feel of the coat, and she thought she would buy it. The woman walked to the mirror and admired herself, turning slowly. When she reached the mirror she posed, turned in a circle and put her hands in the pockets. Suddenly, she felt something sharp pierce her hand and she yelped out in pain. She thought that the sharp object must have been a security tag and she brought her belongings to the front of the store and approached the registers. Minutes later, while on the checkout line, the shopper fell down in front of the cashier. Customers and employees rushed to her aid, only to find that she was already dead.

31

Later when the warehouse of the store was investigated, detectives found eggs, and baby snakes nesting in the warm pockets of the coats.

On college campus', during the week of finals, the dorms have set "quiet hours" so that people can study without being disturbed. Tradition has it that on the last night of finals at 12:00am everyone opens their windows and screams for exactly one minute.

On most campuses you can hear someone tell the story that one year, between 12:00 and 12:01am, a girl was brutally raped and murdered and no one heard her scream for help because of the traditional racket put on by the rest of the Military student body.

Now, according to the story, any one who screams during finals week will be expelled from the school. A Perfect GPA

Many students have been told, and unquestioningly believe, that if your roommate dies you will get a 4.0 grade point average for the rest of the semester (or the rest of the four years you are in college).

The Body in the Bed

A man and his wife were vacationing in Las Vegas and as they arrived in their room they found it was filled with an overpowering stench. They called the front desk to complain, and headed for the casinos for some late-night gambling while the problem was taken care of. When they returned to the room, the stench was replaced with the strong smell of chemical cleaners and deodorizers, annoyed but satisfied that it was better than before they went to bed. Early in the morning the smell had returned so strongly that it awakened them, the man called the manager and angrily demanded another room immediately. While his wife packed up their stuff the man ripped the sheets off the bed, where the smell seemed to be coming from. He found that the mattress had been cut open and a well-dressed corpse had been shoved inside. The couple were given a complimentary suite and free passes to the shows.

The Ultimate Urban Legends

The Keg

A couple had just moved into a small castle they'd recently purchased and were excitedly searching all the nooks and crannies. In a large underground room they found many empty barrels that had been tapped years ago, and one that appeared to be full. They immediately tapped it to find that it contained a delicious brandy.

They drank and served it at parties enjoying not only its flavour, but that it could have been hundreds of years old. Months later when the barrel ran dry, they noticed it was still too heavy to be empty, they cut it open and found a shrivelled corpse curled up in the barrel.

- This one's especially interesting because sometimes bodies were shipped this way to preserve them for burial.

Made in Usa

In the 50's a town in Japan was renamed Usa so that products could be shipped to the US with the stamp MADE IN USA . - There is a city in Japan named Usa, but it's been there for much longer.

The Cranbury Inn

I lived in NJ most of my life, even though I was born in NY. When I went to Walter C. Black Middle School, I had a teacher who worked at the Cranbury Inn.

She told us all that it was haunted by the ghost of a man who was killed there in the 1790's. The man was run over by a stagecoach after having a few too many drinks. Apparently, ever since then he has been haunting the place he died, especially when the owners tried to renovate. Military As it was told, while my teacher was working there, the kitchen was beginning to be remodelled, and suddenly pots and pans started coming right out of the cabinets and striking people! I did hear that quite some time ago, so the preciseness of my memory may not be exact, but I assure you, that there is certainly something haunting the Cranbury Inn in Cranbury, NJ.

The Chat room

A young boy met a new friend in a chat room and began talking to him regularly, the friend was from out of state but would be in town in a couple weeks and they made plans to sneak out and meet. The boy began to feel odd about the arrangement and confessed the whole thing to his father. The father contacted the authorities and after a couple hours the chat was traced to a local prison, the prisoner who'd been using that computer was scheduled for release in two weeks.

The Concerned Mother

A man and wife were driving late one night when they were flagged down by a woman that appeared to be hurt. She claimed she'd been in an accident and her baby was alive but trapped in the car. The man told her to wait with his wife and he'd see what he could do. He got to the car and found a couple obviously dead in the front seat but a baby crying in a car seat. He cut the baby loose and returned to his own car. When he got there his wife was alone, he asked her where the woman had went and she replied that she'd followed him to the wreck. He left the baby with his wife and went back to the car to find her. When he got there he realized the woman who'd been instantly killed in the front seat had been the one who'd flagged him down.

The Graveyard Wager

A group of young girls were having a slumber party one night and began to exchange ghost stories. One girl claimed that the old man who had been buried earlier that week in the graveyard down the street had been buried alive. She claimed that if you tried you could hear him scratching at the lid of his coffin still. The other girls called her bluff and told her she was afraid to go there tonight. She eventually accepted their challenge and took a stake with her to drive in the ground to prove she'd been there. She headed off to the gravesite right away and never returned the others assumed she had "chickened out" and went home ashamed. The next morning as they passed the graveyard they saw her there at the old man's grave. She had accidentally staked her nightshirt to the ground and died of fright.

The Hairy Hitchhiker

A young lady driving alone down the highway one night says a large grey-haired woman slowly walking along the side of the road. She pulled over and offered the old woman a ride. As they rode along, the women made small-talk. As the old lady offered her a stick of gum, she noticed the old woman's hands were very wide and the knuckles were badly scarred, she also saw how incredibly hairy the woman's arm was. Realizing her mistake, she swerved and said she thought she'd hit something, then she stopped and asked the old lady if she'd take a look. When the old lady was behind the car, the girl sped off. The young girl immediately felt guilty realizing that she had probably just been an old woman, and in her nervousness she had behaved very badly. She felt even worse when she notices the old woman's purse sitting in the floor of the passenger side. Realizing she couldn't just go on with it, she lifted it from the floor and saw that inside it was filled with wallets, watches and jewellery and a large bloody hunting knife.

The Hitchhiking Prophet

During World War II a couple were driving home one night and picked up a hitchhiker. The man barely spoke during the ride, but as he got out he thanked the couple and told them to repay their kindness, he'd answer any question they may ask. The driver smiled and said "Allright, when will the war end?" the hitchhiker replied

"The war will end in July as surely as you will have a dead man in your car before you get home." Unsettled, the couple said good-bye and drove off. Before they reached home they saw a wrecked ambulance by the road, they picked up the driver and a badly hurt patient. By the time they reached the hospital, the patient had already died. As the shock wore off, the couple regretted that they hadn't asked the hitchhiker what year.

All Apologies

A man making a late-night stop at a convenience store came out and found his car had been stolen. The next day the owner of the convenience store calls him and tells him to come back right away. When he gets there he finds his car is back in the exact space it had been stolen from, on the dash in a note that says "Sorry for any inconvenience, my wife was having a baby and I had to take her to the hospital." Relieved but annoyed, the man phones the police to tell them then returns home. When he gets there he finds that everything in his home has been stolen. On the table is a note that says, "Sorry for any inconvenience, but I have to put my kids through college, don't I?"

Beam Me Up, Scotty

An amateur pilot was arrested in the UK for flying under Tower Bridge in London. When contacted by the Air Traffic Controllers he identified himself as Captain James T. Kirk of the Starship Enterprise. When he was asked if he wanted to say anything on his own behalf before the judge passed sentence, he pretended his wallet was a Star Trek communicator, whistled, and said "Beam me up Scotty, I'm in the shit."

Gnome Come Home

A lady looked out her window one morning to discover her lawn gnomes were missing. She called the police and they came and looked around, but told her not to expect much. A few days later she got a postcard in the mail from Hawaii that read: "We decided to take a vacation. Having a wonderful time, wish you were here. The Gnomes." Two weeks later she answered the doorbell to find the gnomes standing on the porch.

Good Neighbours

A young couple moved into a part of town where most of their neighbours were of Italian descent. One day they came home and found they had been robbed. They went to ask their neighbour, an older Italian man, if he'd seen anything. He told them he didn't, but not to call the police yet. He seemed to know what he was talking about, and they didn't want to offend him, so they decided to wait until evening to report it. A couple hours later there was a knock at the door, and all of their stolen belongings were sitting neatly at the steps.

The Kidney Heist

Three young men were spending the weekend partying in a popular tourist-town in Mexico. One of the men left the bar with an attractive lady, saying he'd see the guys the next day. The next evening the other men began to worry about their friend, and went to his room to check on him. After breaking in they found him on the bed, unconscious and bleeding. They found a fresh surgical closure on his back and called for an ambulance. At the hospital they were shocked to discover one of his kidneys had been removed.

This one takes place in alot of towns, mostly in South America, but sometimes as close as New York. The doctor sometimes comments that it happens all the time, they sell the organs on the black market.

The Kind Stranger

An older man who never learned to read or write met a stranger in a bar one afternoon. After about two hours the stranger asked his new friend if he could do him a favour. He wanted him to go to the betting shop across the road and put some money on a horse that was running that afternoon. When the man explained he was illiterate and he couldn't write out a docket the stranger said it was ok as he already had one written out. So the man went to the betting shop and handed in the docket. When the teller took the docket from him and read it she screamed help and dived on the ground. The man was standing at the counter bewildered when all of a sudden five regular customers from the betting shop set upon him and began to beat him. Then the police were called and the man

37

was arrested. When he asked why he was being arrested when he was the one that was attacked and they told him it was for attempted robbery and he could expect a long spell in prison. When he asked how they had come to that conclusion they read the docket to him which read "This is a robbery I have a gun, give me all the money". When he explained about the stranger the police checked it out but no one could be found fitting that description in the bar.

The Lie Detector

Some Policemen were interrogating an unintelligent but particularly stubborn suspect one day when one of them had a bright idea. He wheeled in a copy machine with a metal mixing-bowl wired to it, and said "If you're telling the truth, you won't mind taking a little lie-detector test." Worried, but seeing no alternative but giving it a try, the suspect agreed. Each time the suspect gave an answer that was obviously a lie, the policeman made a copy of the sheet he'd already put in the copier that said: "LIE". Realizing he couldn't fool the machine, the criminal eventually gave in, confessing and telling the officers all they needed to know.

This one was done in an episode of NYPD Blue and Homicide: Life on the Street.

The Smuggler's Baby

Drug smuggler's often use hollowed-out dead babies to smuggle drugs across the border.

State Police Don't Have Balls

As a young woman was being written a citation for speeding she asked the police officer if she couldn't just buy a couple of tickets to the policeman's ball instead. The policeman replied, "I'm sorry Miss, state policemen don't have balls." The troopers face turned red, he tore up the ticket and drove away.

The Toothbrushes

Young honeymooners at a popular vacation spot returned to their room one evening to find that it had been robbed. Everything in the room was stolen except for their toothbrushes and camera. Knowing that the honeymoon was more important than anything that had been taken, they used credit cards to replace the stolen items, and went on about enjoying themselves. A couple weeks after their return they got their photos back and sat down to look through them together. They were enjoying their photos until they got to the one that was taken in the hotel room of a large hairy man with their toothbrushes stuck in his rear-end.

The Two Hitchhikers

A salesman driving along the highway one day saw a hitcher and decided picking him up would be a good way to relieve his boredom. After he did, he immediately regretted it, the man was large and menacing, and his questions about the salesman's business quickly made him nervous. Ahead he saw another hitchhiker and decided his best bet was to pick this one up too, especially since this one was well dressed and very clean-cut.

As soon as the second hitcher got in the back seat he pointed a gun at the two men in the front and demanded their valuables. The front-seat passenger swung his arm back and smashed the robber in the head with his elbow, knocking him unconscious. Before the salesman could even say anything, the large man took the gun and all the unconscious robbers' possessions and pushed him back out of the car. As he turned to the salesman, gun in hand, the salesman begged him not to hurt him, he'd do whatever the large man wanted. The large hitchhiker said: "Relax buddy, I'm not gonna rob you, it's my day off."

Who Threw the Ham?

A large woman was shoplifting at a grocery store when a ham fell out of her overcoat. She looked around indignantly and yelled, "Alright, who threw a ham at me?"

Two-Striped Telamonia

The Ultimate Urban Legends

A spider bite...please read........... And you thought the brown recluse was bad!!!

Three women in North Florida turned up at hospitals over a 5-day period, all with the same symptoms. Fever, chills, and vomiting, followed by muscular collapse, paralysis, and finally, death. There were no outward signs of trauma. Autopsy results showed toxicity in the blood. These women did not know each other, and seemed to have nothing in common.

It was discovered, however, that they had all visited the same Restaurant (Olive Garden) within days of their deaths. The health department descended on the restaurant, shutting it down. The water and air conditioning were all inspected and tested, to no avail.

The big break came when a waitress at the restaurant was rushed to the hospital with similar symptoms. She told doctors that she had been on vacation, and had only went to the restaurant to pick up her check. She did not eat or drink while she was there, but had used the restroom. That is Military when one toxicologist, remembering an article he had read, drove out to the restaurant, went into the restroom, and lifted the toilet seat.

Under the seat, out of normal view, was a small spider. The spider was captured and brought back to the lab, where it was determined to be the Two-Striped Telamonia (Telamonia dimidiata), so named because of its reddened flesh colour. This spider's venom is extremely toxic, but can take several days to take effect. They live in cold, dark, damp climates, and toilet rims provide just the right atmosphere. Several days later a lawyer from Jacksonville showed up at a hospital emergency room. Before his death, he told the doctor, that he had been away on business, had taken a flight from Indonesia, changing planes in Singapore, before returning home. He did not visit (Olive Garden), while there. He did, as did all of the other victims, have what was determined to be a puncture wound, on his right buttock. Investigators discovered that the flight he was on had originated in India. The Civilian Aeronautics Board (CAB) ordered an immediate inspection of the toilets of all flights from India, and discovered the Two-Striped Telamonia (Telamonia dimidiata) spider's nests on 4 different planes!

It is now believed that these spiders can be anywhere in the country. So please before you use a public toilet, lift the seat to check for spiders. It can save your life! And please pass this on to everyone you care about.

The Men's Room

While out shopping around the big city with his mom a small boy wants to go pee. She starts to take him to the women's rest room, but he wants to go to the men's room so she lets him go in and stands around waiting outside. Five minutes or so later, a group of youths come out, laughing and snickering, and disappear into the city. Ten minutes go by. She's getting anxious, and stops a chap walking by to ask him if he'll go in and hurry up her boy. He obliges, but promptly staggers out and vomits. Inside, the boy has had his throat cut and his penis and testicles hacked off and shoved in his mouth. - Phantom

The Severed Fingers

A young man and his date were trying to watch a movie at the local drive-in, but they kept being disturbed by a car-load of delinquents next to them. Eventually the boy got up the nerve to ask them to calm down. The delinquents approached them and began shaking the car and trying to open the doors, yelling threats at the young man and his date. Realizing his error the young man started the engine and sped off as quickly as he could. When he got home he noticed there were three severed fingers jammed behind his rear bumper.

Thread the Needle

Three delinquents were out riding their motorcycles late one night, when the leader decided he would scare the others by riding up ahead of them, turning around and speeding back and driving in between them. After he disappeared from sight, a large semi passed the other bikers. The leader came zipping down the highway and instead of going between his friends bikes, he ran straight between the semi's headlights.

Boiled Diver

Fire Authorities in California found a corpse in a burnt out section of forest whilst assessing the damage done by a forest fire. The body was dressed in a full wetsuit, complete with a dive tank, flippers and face mask.

A post-mortem examination revealed that the diver did not die from burns, but from massive internal injuries. Investigators then set about determining how a fully clad diver ended up in the middle of a forest fire. They found that, on the day of the fire, the person went for a diving trip off the coast - some 20 MILES away from the forest.

The fire-fighters, seeking to control the fire as quickly as possible, called in a fleet of helicopters with very large buckets. The buckets were dropped into the ocean for rapid filling, then flown to the forest fire and emptied. The diver was scooped out of the ocean, into the bucket and dropped over the fire.

Apparently, he extinguished exactly 1.78m (5'10") of the fire.

Doctor Appointment

After anthropologist Susan McKinley came back home from an expedition in South America, she noticed a very strange rash on her left breast. Nobody knew what it was and she quickly dismissed it believing that the holes would leave in time. Upon her return she decided to see a doctor after she started developing intense pains. The doctor, not knowing the exact severity of the disease, gave her antibiotics and special creams. As time lapsed the pain did not subside and her left breast became more inflamed and started to bleed. She decided to bandage her sores however as Susan's pain grew more intense she decided to seek help from a more certified doctor.

Dr. Lynch could not diagnose the infection and told Susan to seek the aid of one of his colleagues who specialized in dermatology whom was sadly on vacation. She waited for two weeks and finally was able to react the dermatologist. Sadly, a life changing event was about to unfold appointment. To Miss McKinley's surprise, after she removed the bandages, they found larva growing and squirming within the pores and sores of her breast. Sometimes these wicked creatures would all together simultaneously move around into different crevices. What she didn't know was that the holes were in fact, deeper than she had originally thought for these larvae were feeding off the fat, tissue, and even milk canals of her bosom.

Dog Walker

There was the husband who was in the habit of taking the family dog for a nice long walk each evening. It was good exercise for both of them, his wife felt, and the dog became so used to the routine that it positively drooled to be taken out on schedule every night.

When her husband was sick one evening, the wife took the dog out instead. And to her surprise the dog pulled vigorously at the leash and led her around the Military block to a house around the corner and began to scratch at the door. A female voice called out, "I won't be a minute, darling." Soon the door was opened by an attractive young woman in a negligee, and the dog dashed in straight to a dish of meat that was waiting for him -- as usual.

Don't Look Back

On the foggy night of their senior costume party Nicole and her date Mark were driving to their school in Mark's old 1987 Toyota. They heard a special news report "...warning everyone the convicted killer, Owen the HangMan Helms, has escaped from the near-by criminal asylum he was last seen in a woods by Pinecrest..."

Nicole started freaking out "That's just on the other side of the valley! Mark turn the car around I want to go home" but just then the car bucked twice then died. An overhanging tree branch went THUNK... THUNK... THUNK... on the roof of the car and Nicole jumped. "It's fine. I'm going to look for help" said Mark, "climb in the back and cover yourself up in that blanket. When I come back I'll knock on the roof 3 times. If you hear more or less than 3 knocks DONT OPEN IT UP."

Nicole tried to persuade him not to go but Mark said "What are we going to do? We can't just sit here until someone drives by." and so he left. Nicole locked the car doors and climbed into the back seat and covered herself up in the blanket and waited. She looked at her watch 25 minutes had passed... 35... 40 then she heard a knock... "Oh come on two more" knock... "yes! mark just one more" knock... "ok! stop no more mark please let that be you!" knock... "NO!" her blood turned ice cold knock... knock... knock... "please someone! please! someone help me!" she prayed she thought it might be the Hangman trying to torment her... did he know she was inside?

Then the knocking stopped. She could hear a radio, with a dispatcher's voice giving instructions that she couldn't make out. Two men were staring at her through the window. Nicole realized they were police, behind them she saw the spinning blue and red lights of the police car, "its ok young lady. You can come out now" said the 1st police officer.

Nicole's shaking hand finally found the lock and she stumbled out. "Where's Mark? Didn't he come with you?" Nicole asked. "Come to the patrol car. DONT LOOK BACK - just keep your eyes straight ahead" said the 2nd police officer.

"Why can't I look back?" she asked.

"Just come on to the patrol car miss" said the police men. Then Nicole looked behind her and saw Mark, still in his grey-jogging outfit, hanging from an overhead tree branch. One of his Nike shoes was gently hitting the roof of the car, knock... knock... knock...

Don't Look Back... Another Version

The story is the same up until he leaves the car. He tells his girlfriend to lock the doors and don't open them until he taps on the roof three times. He leaves and she does what he says and was for him to come back.

About an hour goes by and she starts to get worried when she hears tapping on the roof. After three times she is about to open the door, but the tapping doesn't stop. Confused and frightened she doesn't open the door at all and sits in there for hours, the whole time hearing the tapping on the roof.

Finally the police arrived and a cop came to the car and told her to get out, to come with him and not to look back. Of course she does looks back to find her boyfriend hanging from a tree over the car. The wind caused the branch to rock making his feet tap the car over and over,

Deadly Dress

A new consignment boutique opened in town and a woman went shopping there and bought a dress. She wore it that night to a party. Sometime during the party the woman began to feel sick. She had had a few cocktails, so she thought it was just a reaction to the alcohol. She said her goodbyes and headed home. That night, alone in her apartment she felt worse and worse and by morning she had died in her bathroom, still wearing her party dress.

In the morgue during the autopsy, the examiner recognized the dress from Military another body that had been brought in weeks before. He had embalmed that body while she was wearing the dress. Later, he removed the dress from the body and sold it to a man he knew who owned a consignment shop.

The examiner realized that the embalming fluid had soaked into the dress. When the woman bought the dress and wore it to the party, she exposed herself to the embalming fluid which then absorbed into her and had been the cause of her death.

Eddie Murphy in an Elevator

The Ultimate Urban Legends

An older woman took her first trip to Las Vegas last year. She had done very well playing the slot machines, winning a bucket full of quarters. Karen needed a break, and she left the casino heading toward the elevators, taking her bucket with her.

She steps into the elevator and before the doors shut, four beefy, leather-clad African-American men step in. Karen (never having spent much time with African Americans) clutches her bucket close to her body.

One of the men says, "Hit the floor, lady," and she does: quarters fly everywhere. The men bust up laughing and they help Karen collect her winnings. One of the men explains that he meant for her to select her floor. They help her collect her quarters and the elevator arrives at her floor. She leaves embarrassed, and the men are still laughing.

Later that evening, a dozen roses are delivered to Karen's room. There Military is a one hundred dollar bill attached to each rose. The note attached read:

Thank you for the best laugh I've had in years! Eddie Murphy

Variations:

The celebrity can be either Eddie Murphy, Michael Jordan or Reggie Jackson. The story takes place in New York City, Las Vegas or Atlantic City. Sometimes the man is alone, other times he has bodyguards.

The story has been told where the man has a dog named "Lady." Instead of saying "hit the floor," he says "sit Lady," referring to the dog. Depending on the version of the story, the woman finds her hotel bill taken care of instead of a bouquet of roses.

Don't Lick Envelopes

We received this submittal as a group of stories and testimonials on why you should avoid licking envelopes from now on. As if anyone uses "snail mail" anymore...kidding, kidding... I used to work for an envelope company. Our plant supervisor used to work in the Chicago plant and told us not to lick the envelopes because they would often find dead rats at the bottom of the glue barrel (after thousands of envelopes had been glued and shipped). EEWW!

I work in a factory and we have 2 employees who used to work in an envelope factory. They told me that when the machine jams up, they use whatever water is handy to thin out the glue. This includes water that they just mopped the floor Military with. Since then, I've avoided licking envelopes.

If you lick your envelopes... You won't anymore! A woman was working in a post office in California. One day she licked the envelopes and postage stamps instead of using a sponge. That very day the lady cut her tongue on the envelope. A week later, she noticed an abnormal swelling of her tongue. She went to the doctor, but they found nothing wrong. Her tongue was not sore or anything. A couple of days later, her tongue started to swell more, and it began to get so sore, that she could not eat.

She went back to the hospital, and demanded something be done.

The doctor took an x-ray of her tongue and noticed a lump. He prepared her for minor surgery. When the doctor cut her tongue open, a live cockroach crawled out! There were roach eggs on the seal of the envelope. The egg was able to hatch inside of her tongue, because of her saliva. It was warm and moist. This is a true story reported on CNN.

Andy Hume wrote: "Hey, I used to work in an envelope factory. You wouldn't believe the things that float around in those gum applicator trays. I haven't licked an envelope for years!"

To All: I used to work for a print shop (32 years ago) and we were told NEVER to lick the envelopes. I never understood why until I had to go into storage and pull out 2500 envelops that were already printed for a customer who was doing a mailing and saw several squads of roaches roaming around inside a couple of boxes with eggs everywhere. They eat the glue on the envelopes. I think print shops have a harder time controlling roaches than a restaurant. I always buy the self-sealing type. Or if need be, I use a glue stick to seal one that has the type of glue that needs to be wet to stick.

Anonymous in NJ

A little research on the subject reveals that roach eggs are actually laid in batches and stored in an egg case. Depending on the species, each egg case can hold as many as 52 individual eggs and the eggs cannot survive outside this case. Therefore, if the story were true, the hapless victim would have ended up with a mouth full of the critters rather than just one. Also, the egg cases are quite large, and even if one did end up on the lickable portion of the envelopment, it is quite unlikely that the person doing the licking would not have noticed it!

What's more, the claim that the story was reported on CNN appears to be false. A search of the CNN site reveals no mention of the story.

Fallen Baby

In the town of Wentzeville, MO. it is said that in the early 1800's a young mother rode her horse into town with her infant son in a sling on her back. She stayed too late in town and it was past dark when she set out to return home.

As she made her way home, the sky clouded over and she could hear distant thunder as a storm approached. The road was very dark without the moonlight and she began to notice rustling Military noises coming from the darkness all around her. The girl began to look over her shoulder in panic as she became more and more aware of how alone she was. As the chills crawled up her spine, she hoped that the child wouldn't sense her fear. Suddenly she heard a scream only a few feet from her horse. She became so frightened that she spurred her horse into a fast run. As the horse fled, all the jarring caused the baby to be thrown from her back. The young woman was so horrified she couldn't think, she urged the horse faster and faster away from the sound, further and further away from the child.

Later the mother returned, sick with guilt, to search for the fallen baby. Though the storm had passed, the moonlight revealed no clues to the young woman. Her child had disappeared in the night.

To this day they say if you stop on this lonely stretch of road just before a storm you can hear a loud scream, then the sound of horse's hooves, and then a baby crying.

Fatal Tan

It was the day before a couple's wedding. The bride to be wanted to look beautiful in her white wedding dress so she went to a local salon to get a "healthy looking" tan. Afterward, she felt like she was still pretty pale so she lathered herself up with deep tanning lotion and visited every tanning salon in her town.

The next day, right after the couple said "I do", the bride fell over dead. The autopsy reported that her organs had been cooked ten times.

Sandra's house.

There are two girls and one is spending the night at the other's house for one full weekend. One is totally fearless and the other frightens when you tap her on the shoulder - lets call them Marie and Sandra (Sandra is the fearless one and Marie is the wimp).

They sleepover at Sandra's house. Sandra has a million horror movies but because Marie is scared of seeing gore they decide to tell each other ghost stories. Sandra is the expert on any type of frightening story and she really wants to scare Marie. She tells her stories of babysitters hacked to death, eaten alive and all sorts of terrible happenings. Military By now they have consumed a lot of water and popcorn so after her last story Sandra excuses herself to the bathroom. Minutes passed and all Marie could think of were the stories she had just heard. When Marie heard no running water she began to worry.

Logically thinking that Sandra was playing an elaborate joke, Marie waited again. Sandra's phone rang and Marie jumped. The phone rang again and again so she assumed that Sandra was unable to answer it so Marie picked it up. "Hello?" she said nervously. All she heard was breathing at the other end then a click.

Marie began to panic. She climbed into Sandra's bed and put the covers over her head. When she finally heard the scuffling of feet she assumed they were Sandra's but the shuffling passed by the door and did not pause. Marie was too frightened to call out Sandra's name so she waited. Eventually she heard the feet again but they seemed very far away. Then a scream let out across the house.

Marie was very shaken now. She wasn't sure if it was Sandra messing with her head or if someone was really going through the house. Marie finally mustered up the courage and began to wander around the vast house. All the lights were out except for the glowing of Sandra's room light and the light of the moon outside.

Marie began to inch down the hallway praying that this was some giant hoax. Finally she turned a corner and saw Sandra sitting at the end of the hall. Her pajamas were red and she seemed to be leaning against the wall. Marie sighed. The fear was gone. She knew it was just Sandra messing with her head.

She flicked on the nearest light switch and to her horror Sandra was kneeling against the wall but she was covered in blood, her eyes were gouged out, and her stomach was ripped open. Marie let out a terrified scream as she read the words painted in Sandra's own blood over her mutilated corpse. "She became her own Urban Legend".

Bookkeeper in a Brothel

A very rich, self-made business man was being chased by a magazine that wished to honour him. He told the reporter that when he'd first came to the city he'd tried to get a job as a bookkeeper in a brothel, but had been kicked out when the Madam realized he couldn't read or write. On the streets he began selling fruit, then later opened a grocery, then a whole string of grocery stores all across the country. At the end of the the reporter was shocked to learn the man still couldn't read or write and said "Wow, just imagine what you'd have become if you'd learned to read and write." The business man replied "Well, I expect I'd have been a bookkeeper in a whorehouse."

The Cabbage Patch Tragedy

A woman washed cabbage in the washing machine and damaged it badly. Since they were so difficult to come buy she sent it back to the company hoping it could be repaired. A few weeks later she received a death- certificate in the mail, and a bill for the funeral.

The Dishonest Note

A man returned from shopping to find his car had been badly dented, and the culprit was no where in sight. As he got closer he felt relieved when he saw a note had been placed under his windshield-wiper. Laughing at himself for doubting the honesty of the average person, he pulled the note loose and read it, it said:"THE PEOPLE WATCHING ME THINK I'M LEAVING MY NAME AND ADDRESS, BUT I'M NOT."

The Fart in the Car

A woman was very nervous about her first date with a man she'd been attracted to for a long time. When he came to her door, she started to feel gassy and realized the chilli she'd had for lunch had been a bad idea. Being a gentleman, he carefully put her in the car and shut the door for her, as he walked around to his side; she farted loudly and quickly opened the window and began fanning. She was horrified when he got in and pointed to the back seat saying "Have you met Ruth and Bob?"

Old vs Young

An old lady was waiting for a car to pull out of a parking space at a crowded grocery store one day. When the car pulled out another car pulled in front of her, and into the space. The teenager hopped out of the car and said to the old woman, "I'm younger and faster, lady." The old lady sits there for a second, then rams the kid's car. As she backs up and gets ready to drive away she tells the teenager: "I'm older and better insured, kid."

Red Handed

A drunk driver was pulled over by a police officer late one night. As he was trying to walk a straight line, there was a crash from a nearby alley and the policeman told the drunk to wait while he checked it out. After waiting about ten minutes the drunk decided it was silly to wait, and drove home. The next morning the police officer knocked on his door. The driver stuck to the story that he'd been at home all evening and the policeman demanded he open the garage door. The man obliged wondering what the policeman hoped to find. He realized his mistake when he saw the police car in his garage.

The policeman's often so embarrassed by the situation that he doesn't press charges. This story was told in "Good Will Hunting".

Gang Lights

If you are driving after dark and see an on-coming car with no headlights on, DO NOT FLASH YOUR LIGHTS AT THEM! This is a common gang member "initiation game" that goes like this:

The new gang member under initiation drives along with no headlights, and the first car to flash their headlights at him is now his "target". He is now required to turn around and chase that car, and shoot at or into the car in order to complete his initiation requirements. Make sure you share this information with all the drivers in your family!

Gas Boycott

Gas rationing in the 80's worked even though we grumbled about it. It might even be good for us! The Saudis are boycotting American goods. We should return the favour.

Every time you fill up the car, you can avoid putting more money into the coffers of Saudi Arabia. Just buy from gas companies that don't import their oil from the Saudis.

I thought it might be interesting for you to know which oil companies are the best to buy gas from and which major companies import Middle Eastern oil:

Disturbing

Several years ago, "they" say, Mr. Gere was admitted into the emergency room of a Los Angeles hospital with a gerbil lodged in his rectum. Gere was alone when he arrived, some say, or with a partner (e.g., former girlfriend Cindy Crawford) according to others. It took a whole team of surgeons to extract the animal from Gere's posterior. Some variants say the gerbil was found to have been shaven and declawed; others claim the animal had been placed in a special plastic pouch. And some say the poor creature was Gere's own beloved pet, aptly named "Tibet." In any case, when the surgery was finally done the team was sworn to secrecy (unsuccessfully, we must conclude) and Gere went on his merry way, suffering no permanent damage other than to his reputation. The requested URL /madmen/gotaway.html was on this server.

Gravity Hill

This is my own experience with Gravity Hill in Jackson NJ.

A friend of mine from work lived in Jackson and I drove her home one night when we got out of work late. She wanted to show me "Gravity Hill" which was close to where she lived. On the way to Jackson, she told me a story about a teenaged girl named Helen who lived with her father. Her mother had died when she was very young and her father raised her. He was a truck driver and would sometimes have to leave town for days at a Military time. Helen was used to being home alone.

One night a man came to their door and asked for help. He was having car trouble and needed a place to stay so Helen's father offered their couch for the night.

The next morning Helen woke to find her father gone. The stranger tried to calm her and tell her that he had left to go on a long haul. He told her that her dad had said he could stay as long as he liked. Helen grew suspicious and felt the man had hurt, or possibly killed her dad! She argued with the man and when he charged at her she ran for her life out of the house. As she passed the hall table, she grabbed her father's keys to the car in the driveway. Somehow, she started the car and pulled out onto the road but they lived on a hill and when she shifted the car into drive to make her escape, she stalled just as the man burst through the front door and began to cross the lawn.

Helen was terrified and thought she would be caught for sure when suddenly, the ghost of her father who had been murdered by the stranger during the night, pushed her car up the hill. She was able to start the car and escape the man who killed her father.

During the last part of the story, we had been driving down some secluded streets without any streetlights. When she finished telling the tale I had stopped the car at a stop sign and was waiting for her to tell me which way to turn. All she said was "Ok, now put the car in neutral and take your foot off the brake."

I was driving a 1985 Lincoln Town car and it had a digital speedometer. I realized we were there. We were facing the bottom of the hill! I shifted into neutral and lifted my foot. The car rolled slowly up the hill - backwards - and the digital Additional gauge read 1 mile per hour. We rolled uphill approx. 30 ft and then just hovered there for a few seconds before I threw the car into drive and found us some streetlights!

Another Version - Spook Hill

There is a place in MT Cotton Brisbane Australia that everyone calls Spook Hill. You apparently have to stop your car halfway up the deadened road and turn your car off and put it in neutral. your car then rolls uphill by itself. It is said that that where killed in a bus accident push the car up and you can hear feet scrambling beside your car.

Another story is the magnetism in the mountains is high there and that can pull a car up the hill.

A couple of towns over in an area outside of Boonesboro off route 67, there is a small town that prides itself on civil war heritage. You can put your car in neutral on "spook hill" and the ghosts of civil war soldiers will push it up the hill thinking it is cannon. All the local teenagers try it some even putting flour on their freshly washed to verify the existence of ghostly handprints.

Hamster Mishap

A boy was playing with his hamster in the basement of his house just before the carpet man came to put new carpet down. When he arrived the boy's mom told him to go upstairs and let the carpet man work in peace. It was a large basement and after a while the carpet man was exhausted and decided to go out for a smoke.

He saw a lump under the carpet he just laid down and realized that his cigarette pack was missing. Instead of pulling up the carpet and lying it down again he just hammered the little lump down.

On his way home after a long day, he found his cigarettes in his truck. He was wondering what the little lump in the floor was so he called the lady of the house the next day and ask her if she was missing any small items. She was surprised to hear from him and told him that they hadn't been able to find her son's hamster since the day before. ,

The Hanging Tree

In Brazoria, TX two slaves were unjustly hung by the neck from the limb of an old sturdy tree until they died. The ghosts of the slaves have haunted that area ever since.

In the past, drivers of horse pulled wagons they said that their horses would just stop below the tree.A man who didn't believe the tales coaxed his horse under the tree and the animal stopped in its tracks. He had to force his horse to leave the spot. Now they say that a car driven under the branches of that old tree will stall every time.

There is a church not to far from the tree and one night a woman was walking home from the church when she heard a noise. She turned and saw a small black boy a few yards behind her. She asked him if he needed help, but he didn't reply so she turned and started walking again. When she looked back moments later, she saw the figure had grown to a boy of about 12 and was following her soundlessly.

She began to walk faster and when she looked again the boy was a teenager. She began running from him and when she panicked and looked back again a grown man was close behind her. She ran to a nearby home and crashed through their front door while they were cheerfully eating dinner. The man had disappeared.

Stand under that tree at night and the boy will appear to you too.

Haunted Gym

There is a ghost who haunts Charles Page High School in Sand Springs, OK 40 years ago, there was some construction being done in the gymnasium of the High School. There was an accident and the roof collapsed. One of the workers fell 60 feet through the ceiling and died that tragic day. The spirit of this worker haunts the school and has been the cause of a high turnover in the janitorial staff. Custodians come and go, many quit when they encounter the spirit who makes his appearances mostly in the school gymnasium, where he fell. There is a soft, indented spot, on the gym floor where the man fell. .They say strange sounds can be heard when the spirit is around, like doors opening and closing and locking by themselves. Basketballs can be heard bouncing on the floor, when there aren't any around and voices seem to be coming from the musty air in the gym.

The Ultimate Urban Legends

The Haunted School

There is this school called "The Institute That Must Not Be Named" (a real school, and hey we don't want to get sued here) that is in Danvers Massachusetts. Legend has it that it was actually built right over the real place where they buried the witches who were killed in the Salem witch trials. It used to be a part of Olde Salem. It is a school for people studying to be vets, plant nursery workers, etc., so there are a lot of animals and plants there. A lot of strange things happen and a lot of people get hurt. Animals will get spooked by something no one else can see. People will be working with a plant and then it looks as though someone has stepped on it when no one else is there. People have also said they have been walking in a really warm spot and then it just get's cold. And people have seen things...like balls of light floating around in dark areas, doors that fly open even if they are locked, windows that open and shut and the blinds on the windows that have been pulled have been known to come flying up. The worst thing that happened was when one of the students, he was a senior, was standing alone near the window on the third floor of the building. Suddenly he started screaming "Leave me alone! I didn't do anything wrong I'm sorry! I'm sorry!!" A teacher ran out of a nearby classroom and saw him swing his fists at the air, and then it seemed as though he was lifted up off of the floor and he went flying out the window. He didn't survive the fall and the doctors had said he died before he had hit the ground. The teacher claims that in the moments she witnessed, she saw a reddish flash out or the corner of her eye, but when she looked directly towards the source of the light, nothing was there.

No other strange deaths have occurred here, but weird things still happen. Now there is a mental house, and a police station, IN the school.

Heavy Cadillac

A driver of a ready-mix concrete truck left for work one day in a bit of a hurry. Later in the morning he realized he had forgotten his lunch, so he decided to simply stop by his house during a delivery and pick it up. As he approached the house, he noticed a strange, new Cadillac parked in the driveway. Curious, he entered quietly by the back door, tiptoed toward the bedroom where he heard his wife and a strange male voice. Just as quietly, he left the house and walked to his truck. He simply backed the truck up to the car, and poking the chute through an open window, filled the car with wet cement. He called his office on the mobile radio, confessed, and offered to pay for the concrete. Amid uproarious laughter, he was told that load was on the company! He drove away, leaving the car flat on the ground.

Later, the man found out that the Cadillac was to be a gift to him from his wife Military and the male voice he heard was the car dealer finalizing the deal. Celebrity Heckler

The setting was a rock concert for the Grand Funk Railroad. After playing for some time, just after a featured guitar solo, someone near the front of the crowd was booing loudly. In response to the booing, a member of the band came to the mike and asked, "If you think you can do better, come on up here."

Up walks Eric Clapton.

Homeless Assist

A woman had just finished grocery-shopping when a group of homeless offered to help her to her car. After loading her groceries one of the asked the woman for a tip, gratefully she obliged.

As she was about to drive off a man ran up to her and told her to go directly to the police station. One of the men had locked himself in the trunk of her car planning to ambush her later with a knife.

Horse Trailer

A man who was always fond of horse racing owned a few horses himself. One of his horses was quite old, but the man decided to race it one last time. The man tried to lead the horse into the mini trailer attached to his truck but the horse wouldn't go in. Finally, after he forced the horse in, he began to drive to the track, a few miles from where he boarded the horse.

The horse was constantly making noise and wouldn't be quiet. The man thought it was just he horse being stubborn. The man then noticed that people were Military honking their car horns at him as they drove by but he ignored the other motorists and kept driving. He knew the horse was upset and wanted to get him out of the trailer as soon as possible.

When he reached the place the racetrack and opened the trailer, he was shocked by what he found. His old horse was dead and the trailer was soaked with blood. The horse's legs had fallen through the rotted floor and were ground to stubs.

Ding!!

An old lady was asked to look after her neighbours Terrier dog, and being the kind-hearted lady she was, she agreed. When taking the dog for a long walk, it started to rain, hurrying back, the old woman returned home, both her and the Terrier were soaked. The poor little animal was shivering, and wanting to dry the dog, she decided to put the animal in the microwave for a short time. When the dog was put inside, the lady's phone rang, and upon answering, she was hooked into a conversation with her friend who had been in hospital. When she ended the call, the microwave was still on. As she opened the microwave door, all that was left of the dog was a gory mess.

Human's Can Lick Too

Once there was a beautiful young girl who lived in a small town just south of Farmersburg. Her parents had to go to town for a while, so they left their daughter home alone, but protected by her dog, which was a very large collie. The parents told the girl to lock all the windows and doors after they had left. And at about 8:00pm the parents went to town. So doing what she was told the girl shut and locked evey window and every door. But there was one window in the basement that would not close completely.

Trying as best as she could she finally got the window shut, but it would not lock. So she left the window, and went back upstairs. But just to make sure that no one could get in, she put the dead-bolt lock on the basement door.

Then she sat down had some dinner and decided to go to sleep for the night. Settling down to sleep at about 12:00 she snuggled up with the dog and fell asleep.

But at one point, she suddenly woke up. She turned and looked at the clock...it was 2:30. She snuggled down again wondering what had woken her.....when she heard a noise. It was a dripping sound. She thought that she had left the water running, and now it was dripping into the drain of her sink. So thinking it was no big deal she decided to go back to sleep. But she felt nervous so she reached her hand over the edge of her bed, and let the dog lick her hand to feel safe, knowing he would protect her. Again at about 3:45 she woke up hearing dripping. She was slightly angry now but went back to sleep anyway. Again she reached down and let the dog lick her hand. Then she fell back to sleep.

At 6:52 the girl decided that she had had enough...she got up just in time to see her parents were pulling up to the house. "Good," she thought. "Now somebody can fix the sink...'cause I know I didn't leave it running." She walked to the bathroom and there was the collie dog, skinned and hung up on the curtain rod.

The noise she heard was its blood dripping into a puddle on the floor. The girl screamed and ran to her bedroom to get a weapon, in case someone was still in the house.....and there on the floor, next to her bed she saw a small note, written in blood, and saying: HUMANS CAN LICK TOO MY BEAUTIFUL. Modern Myths

The Jersey Devil

The Jersey Devil, the supposed mythical creature of the New Jersey Pinelands, has haunted New Jersey and the surrounding areas for the past 260 years. This entity has been seen by over 2,000 witnesses over this period. It has terrorized towns and caused factories and to close down, yet many people believe that the Jersey Devil is a legend, a mythical beast that originated from the folklore of the New Jersey Pine Barrens. Others disagree with this point of view. The following text will show there is evidence to support the existence of an animal or supernatural being known as the Jersey Devil. The evidence consists of the stories of the Jersey Devil's origin, the sightings of it, and finally, the theories on it. Military There are many different versions of the birth of the Jersey Devil. One of the most popular legends says a Mrs. Shrouds of Leeds Point, NJ made a wish that if she ever had another child, she want it to be a devil. Her next child was born misshapen and deformed. She sheltered it in the house, so the curious couldn't see him. On stormy night, the child flapped its arms, which turned into wings, and escaped out the chimney and was never seen by the family again. A Mrs. Bowen of Leeds point said, "The Jersey Devil was born in the Shrouds house at Leeds Point.

Another story that also placed the birth at Leeds Point said that a young girl fell in love with a British soldier during the Revolutionary War. The people of Leeds Point cursed her. When she gave birth, she had a devil. Some people believe the birth of the devil was punishment for the mistreatment of a minister by the Leeds folk.

Pine Barrens, New Jersey Another story placed the birth in Estelville, NJ. Mrs. Leeds, of Estelville, finding out she was pregnant with her 13th child, shouted, "I hope it's a devil". She got her wish. The child wad born with horns, a tail, wings, and a horse-like head. The creature revisited Mrs. Leeds everyday. She stood at her door and told it to leave. After awhile, the creature got the hint and never returned.

Burlington, NJ, also claims to be the birthplace of the Jersey Devil. In 1735, Mother Leeds was in labour on a stormy night.

Gathered around her were her friends. Mother Leeds was supposedly a witch and the child's father was the devil himself. The child was born normal, but then changed form. It changed from a normal baby to a creature with hooves, a horses head, bat wings and a forked tail. It beat everyone present

Additional and flew up the chimney. It circled the villages and headed toward the pines. In 1740 a clergy exercised the devil for 100 years and it wasn't seen again until 1890.

There are many other versions of the legend. The legends say it was the 6th, 8th, 10th, 12th, or 13th child, it was born normal or deformed, and the mother confined it to the cellar or the attic. Although there are many discrepancies in all of these stories, there are 3 pieces of evidence that tie all of the legends of the Jersey Devil's origin together.

1. The first thing that ties the legends together is the name "Leeds". Whether the mother's name was Leeds or the birth place was Leeds Point, all of the stories include the name Leeds. Alfred Heston, the Atlantic County Historian, believes that the devil could be a Leeds or a Shrouds baby. He discovered that a Daniel Leeds opened land in Great Egg Harbor, NJ, in 1699. His family lived in Leeds Point.

2. He also discovered a Samuel Shrouds, Sr. came to Little Egg Harbor, NJ, in 1735 and lived right across the river from the house of Mother Leeds.

3. The 3rd fact ties in the Burlington story with the others stories. Professor Fred MacFadden of Coppin State College, Baltimore, found that a "devil" was mentioned in writings from Burlington as early as 1735. He also indicated that the word "Burlington" was used to name the area from the city of Burlington to the Atlantic Ocean. This means that the name that is now used for the birthplace such as Leeds point or Estelville, could be the same place referred to in the Burlington Legend.

The origins provide some validity to the existence of the Jersey Devil, but the sightings are the most substantial pieces of evidence. The sightings have been divided up into 3 time periods, pre 1909, January 16-23, 1909, and post 1909.

The Ultimate Urban Legends

From the pre 1909 era, few documented records of sightings still exist. The ones that do confirm the existence of the devil.

In the early 19th century, Commodore Stephen Decatur, a naval hero, was testing cannon balls on the firing range when he saw a strange creature flying across the sky. He fired and hit the creature but it kept right on flying across the field. Joseph Bonaparte, former king of Spain and brother of Napoleon, saw the Jersey Devil in Bordentown, NJ, between 1816 and 1839 while he was hunting. In 1840-41 many sheep and chickens were killed by a creature with a piercing scream and strange tracks. In 1859-94, the Jersey Devil was seen and numerous times and reportedly carried off anything that moved in Haddonfield, Bridgeton, Smithville, Long Branch, Brigantine, and Leeds Point. W.F. Mayer of New York noticed while visiting the Pine Barrens, most of the locals would not venture out after dark. The devil was sighted by George Saarosy, A prominent business man, at the NJ/NY border. This was the last reported sighting before the turn of the century.

New Jersey Devil Artist Rendition In 1903, Charles Skinner, author of American Myths and Legends, claimed that the legend of the devil had run its course and that in the new century; NJ would hear no more of the devil. New Jersey rested easy with that thought for 6 years, until the week of January 16-23. 1909. During this week, the devil would leave his tracks all over South Jersey and Philadelphia. He was seen by over 100 people. This was his largest appearance ever.

It all started early Sunday morning, January 16, 1909. Thack Cozzens of Woodbury, NJ, saw a flying creature with glowing eyes flying down the street. In Bristol, PA, John Mcowen heard and saw the strange creature on the banks of the canal. Patrol James Sackville fired at the creature as it flew away screaming. E.W. Minister, Postmaster of Bristol, PA, also saw a bird- like creature with a horse's head that had a piercing scream. When daylight came, the residents of Bristol found hoof prints in the snow. Two local trappers said they had never seen tracks like those before.

On Monday, the Lowdens of Burlington, NJ, found hoof prints in their yard and around their trash, which was half eaten. Almost every yard in Burlington had these strange hoof prints in them. The prints went up trees, went from of open fields. The same tracks were also found in Columbus, Hedding, Kinhora and Rancocas. A hunt was organized to follow the tracks but the dogs wouldn't follow the trail.

On the 19th the Jersey Devil made his longest appearance of the week. At 2:30 am, Mr & Mrs. Nelson Evans of Gloucester were awakened by a strange noise. They watched the devil from their window for 10 minutes. Mr. Evans described the creature they saw:

It was about three feet and half high, with a head like a collie dog and a face like a horse. It had a long neck, wings about two feet long, and its back legs were like those of a crane, and it had horse's hooves. It walked on its back legs and held up two short front legs with paws on them. It didn't use the front legs at all while we were watching. My wife and I were scared, I tell you, but I managed to open the window and say, 'Shoo', and it turned around barked at me, and flew away.

Tuesday afternoon 2 professional hunters tracked the devil for 20 miles in Gloucester. The trail jumped 5 foot fences and went under 8 inch spaces. The hoof prints were found in more parts of South Jersey. A group of observers in Camden, NJ, saw the devil. It barked at them and then took off into the air.

The next day, a Burlington police officer and the Reverend John Pursell of Pemberton saw the Jersey Devil. Rev. Pursell said, "Never saw anything like it before". Posses in Haddonfield found tracks that ended abruptly. In Collingswood, NJ, a posse watched the devil fly off toward Moorestown. Near Moorestown, John Smith of Maple Shade saw the devil at the Mount Carmel Cemetery. George Snyder saw the devil right after Mr. Smith and their descriptions were identical. In Riverside, NJ, hoof prints were found on roof tops and also around a dead puppy.

On Thursday, the Jersey Devil was seen by the Black Hawk Social Club. He was also seen by a trolley full of people in

Clementon as it circled above them. The witness's descriptions matched others from the days before. In Trenton, Councilman E.P. Weeden heard the flapping of wings and then found hoof prints outside his door. The prints were also found at the arsenal in Trenton. As the day wore on the Trolleys in Trenton and New Brunswick had armed drivers to ward off attacks. The people in Pitman filled churches.

Chickens had been missing all week throughout the Delaware Valley, but when the farmers checked their yards that day, they found their chickens dead, with no marks on them. The West Collingswood Fire Department fired their hose at the devil. The devil retreated at first, but then charged and flew away at the last second.

Later that night, Mrs. Sorbinski of Camden heard a commotion in her yard. She opened the door to see the Jersey Devil standing there with her dog in its grip. She hit the devil with a broom until it let go of her dog and flew away.

She started screaming until her neighbours came over. Two police officers arrived at her house where over 100 people had gathered. The crowd heard a scream coming from Kaigan Hill. The mob ran toward the creature on the hill. The Policed shot at it and the devil flew off into the night. The streets of Camden were empty after this.

On Friday, Camden police officer Louis Strehr saw the Jersey Devil saw the devil drinking from a horses' trough. The school in Mt. Ephraim was closed because no students came in. Mills and factories in Gloucester and Hainesport had to close because none of the employees came to work.

Many New Jersey residents wouldn't leave their houses, even in daylight. Officer Merchant of Blackwood drew a sketch of the creature he saw. His sketch coincided with the descriptions from earlier in the week. Jacob Henderson saw the devil in Salem and described it as having "wings and a tail". The devil was only seen once more in 1909 in February.

Since 1909, the Jersey Devil has continued to be sighted by people all over New Jersey. The number of sightings that have been reported to the authorities has dwindled over the years. This could be attributed to the fact that people don't want to be branded as crazy. Even though the number of reported sightings has dropped, there's still a considerable amount of sightings in the post 1909 era.

In 1927, a cab driver on his way to Salem got a flat tire. He stopped to fix the tire. As he was doing this, a creature that stood upright and was covered with hair, landed on the roof of his cab. The creature shook his car violently. He fled the scene, leaving the tire and jack behind. Phillip Smith, who was known as a sober and honest man, saw the devil walking down the street in 1953. The characteristic screams of the Jersey Devil were heard in the woods near Woodstown, NJ, in 1936. Around 1961, 2 couples were parked in a car in the Pine Barrens. They heard a loud screeching noise outside.

Suddenly the roof of the car was smashed in. They fled the scene, but returned later. Again they heard the loud screech. They saw a creature flying along the trees, taking out huge chunks of bark as it went along.

There have been other sightings since 1909, such as the Invasion of Gibbsboro in 1951. The people there saw the devil over a 2 day period. In 1966, a farm was raided and 31 ducks, 3 geese, 4 cats, and 2 dogs were killed. One of the dogs was a large German Shepard which had its throat ripped out. In 1981, a young couple spotted the devil at Atsion Lake in Atlantic County.

In 1987, in Vineland an aggressive German Shepard was found torn apart and the body gnawed upon. The body was located 25 feet from the chain which had been hooked to him. Around the body were strange tracks that no one could identify.

The sightings and prints are the most substantial evidence that exists. Many of the theories on the Jersey Devil are based upon that evidence. Some theories can be proven invalid, while others seem to provide support for the Jersey Devil's existence.

One theory is that the Jersey Devil is a bird. Mrs. Cassidy of Clayton thought it was an invasion of crowfoot ducks. The crowfoot duck is much too small to be mistaken for the devil. Others believe the devil is really a sand hill crane. The crane used to live in South Jersey until it was pushed out by man. The sand hill crane weighs about 12 lbs., is 4 foot high, and a wingspan of 80 inches. It avoids man but if confronted it will fight. It has a loud scream whooping voice that can be heard at a distance. This could account for the screams heard by witnesses. The crane also eats potatoes and corn. This could account for the raids on crops. This theory doesn't explain, however, the killing of live stock. It also doesn't explain why people described the devil as having a horses head, bat wings and tail, all of which the crane doesn't have.

Professor Bralhopf said that "The tracks were made by some prehistoric animal form the Jurassic period". He believes the creature survived underground in a cavern. An expert from the Smithsonian Institute had a theory about ancient creatures surviving underground. He said the Jersey Devil was a Pterodactyl. The Academy of Natural Sciences could find no record of any creature, living or extinct, that resembles the Jersey Devil.

Jack E. Boucher, author of Absagami Yesteryear, has a theory in which he believes the devil was a deformed child. He thinks Mrs. Leeds had a disfigured child and kept it locked away in the house. She grew sick and couldn't feed the child anymore. It escaped out of hunger and raided local farms for. This doesn't take into account the incredible life span of the devil. The child would have been 174 years old in 1909. It also doesn't account for the sightings of the devil flying.

Only a small amount of the sightings and footprints could be hoaxes. The Jersey Devil has been seen by reliable people such as police, government officials, postmasters, businessman, and other people whose "integrity is beyond question". As for the hoof prints, even if some were hoaxes, there is still no way to explain most of the tracks, especially the ones on roof tops and tracks that ended abruptly as if the creature took wing.

The last theory is the most controversial one. Many people believe that the Jersey Devil could be the very essence of evil, embodied. It is said that the devil is an "uncanny harbinger of war" and appears before any great conflict. The Jersey Devil was sighted before the start of the Civil War. It was also seen right before the Spanish American War and WW I. In 1939, before the start of WW II, Mount Holly citizens were awakened by the noise of hooves on their roof tops. The Devil was seen on December 7, 1941, right before Pearl Harbor was bombed. He was also seen right before the Vietnam War. His possible demonic origins. In 1730, Ben Franklin reported a story about a witchcraft trial near Mt Holly, NJ. One of the origin legends say that Mother Leeds was a witch. The Devil's birth could have been a result of a witches curse.

Other facts support the supernatural theory are the reports of the death of the devil. When Commodore Decatur fired a cannon ball at the devil, it went through him and he was unaffected.

In 1909, a track walker on the electric railroad saw the devil fly into the wires above the tracks. There was a violent explosion which melted the track 20 feet in both directions. No body was found and the devil was seen later in perfect health. In 1957, the Department of Conservation found a strange corpse in a burned out area of the pines. It was a partial skeleton, feathers, and hind legs of an unidentifiable creature. The devil was thought to be dead, but reappeared when the people of New Jersey thought that this time his death was real. Each time he is reported dead, he returns. Sometime this year, the Jersey Devil will be 260 years old. It seems the devil is immortal, which a supernatural being would be. Another thing that supports this theory is the incredible distances the devil could fly in a short period of time. No animal could travel as fast as the devil did in 1909 when he was sighted in South Jersey, Philadelphia, and New York through out the week.

None of these theories can give a definitive answer to what the Jersey Devil was or is, but the sightings prove there is something out there. Whether the Jersey devil is a bird or a demon, is still left to speculation. The people of New Jersey have definitely seen something out there lurking in the Pine Barrens.

Jigsaw Mystery

There was an old lady who lived on her own in a very foggy part of Dartmoor.

She had lived alone for fifteen years, ever since her husband had died in a mysterious car accident. However, the car accident is not my present purpose on which to dwell. You see, this old lady had a passion for jigsaw puzzles, it probably came with the stigma of being alone for she had no family or friends and lived in a very secluded spot. Every night she would sit at her dining room table and work on her current jigsaw puzzle until it was finished, then she would start a new one. Military However, there came a night, a rugged, windy, stormy winter night when she ran out of jigsaw puzzles. She was extremely upset as she had nothing else to do (this was in the days before TV and her radio had no signal in so removed a place). She was just thinking of going up to bed earlier than usual when she heard a thud, as if something had fallen onto the mat from the mail flap.

Intrigued, the old lady hobbled downstairs to find a rectangular parcel had been put through the door and now lay, invitingly, on the mat. She picked it up, carried it upstairs to her dining table and opened it to reveal a new jigsaw puzzle! It had no picture of what it made up on the front but the old lady didn't care. Neither did she care who had sent it, she was just so happy to have another puzzle to do.

It took her about an hour to complete it but as she began the get the entire picture her consternation grew for she saw that the picture being made up was that of the very room in which she now sat. Then, she gasped, for she realised that the woman sitting at the table in the picture with her back to the window was a picture of her!!! Her fingers trembled as she placed the last four pieces of the puzzle to reveal a picture of a crazed madman at the window staring into the room, holding an axe!

The last thing that old lady ever heard was the sound of breaking glass...

Kidneys on the Black Market

The crime begins when a business traveller to buy t-shirts goes to a lounge for a drink at the end of the featuring the black market work day. A person in the bar walks up as they kidney urban legend sit alone and offers to buy them a drink. The last thing the traveller remembers until they wake up in a hotel room bath tub, their body submerged to their neck in ice, is sipping that drink. There is a note taped to the wall instructing them not to move and to call 911. A phone is on a small table next to the bathtub for them to call. to buy t-shirts The business traveller calls 911 who have featuring the Black Market become quite familiar with this crime. Kidney The business traveller is instructed by the 911 Urban Legend operators to very slowly and carefully reaches behind them and feels if there is a tube protruding from their lower back. The business traveller finds the tube and answers, "Yes." The 911 operator tells them to remain still, having already sent paramedics to help.

The operator knows that both of the business traveller's kidneys have been harvested.

Klingerman Virus

This is an alert about a virus in the original sense of the word... one that affects your body, not your hard drive. Scary Virus Killing People.

There have been 23 confirmed cases of people attacked by the Klingerman Virus, a virus that arrives in your real mail box, not your e-mail in box.

Someone has been mailing large blue envelopes, seemingly at random, to people inside the US.

On the front of the envelope in bold black letters is printed, "A gift for you from the Klingerman Foundation."

When the envelopes are opened, there is a small sponge sealed in plastic. This sponge carries what has come to be known as the Klingerman Virus, as public health officials state this is a strain of virus they have not previously encountered.

When asked for comment, Florida police Sergeant Stetson said, "We are working with the CDC and the USPS, but have so far been unable to track down the origins of these letters. The return addresses have all been different, and we are certain a remaining service is being used, making our jobs that much more difficult."

Those who have come in contact with the Klingerman Virus have been hospitalized with severe dysentery. So far seven of the twenty three victims have died. There is no legitimate Klingerman Foundation mailing unsolicited gifts.

If you receive an oversized blue envelope in the mail marked," A gift from the Klingerman foundation", DO NOT open it. Place the envelope in a strong plastic bag or container, and call the police immediately.

The "gift" inside is one you definitely do not want.

Interstate Landing Strips

American interstate highways are designed so that every fifth mile is perfectly straight and flat so that if necessary they can be used as landing strips during wartime.

It's The Law

Driving a car while barefoot is illegal. Sea captains can, by their own authority, perform marriages.

Legal Professions

An undercover police officer must answer yes to "Are you a cop?" to avoid entrapment. - Yeah, that's a good idea.

La Llorana

The Ultimate Urban Legends

In the early 1500's, La Llorana was the prettiest girl in a small town somewhere in Texas. Every man in town wanted to marry her but there was one lucky man she hoped to marry. He befriended the family and courted her for a few years before they were married. In 3 years of marriage they had two sons.

One day before the oldest boys birthday, La Llorana's husband went out to "buy a present." He said goodbye to his wife and and left for town. He was never seen again. There were rumours in town saying that he had left his wife for a Military young mistress. Some say that he was murdered, but no one ever knew the true reason why he left his family. Eventually, she got over the abandonment, and had her heart set on a rich farmer. They soon fell in love. She told her lover that she wanted to get married, but he said they could not. She was in shock, and asked him why, but he would not answer. Later, he confessed that he could not marry her because of her sons.

She was so furious she ran all the way home. She told her boys that they were going to go and take a bath down at the river. The boys slowly entered the shallow part of the Rio Grande, but she had other plans. She told the boys that they were now old enough to go in the deep end, and so they did. As she pretended to wash their hair she firmly pressed on their heads and pushed them under water, she didn't let go till they were dead.

After watching the lifeless bodies of her precious sons float away down the river, she ran to her lover's house and explained what she had done. He couldn't believe it and was disgusted by her actions. He declared that he couldn't love a murderer and told her never to come to his house again.

Suddenly, she realized what she had just done to her family. She ran back to the river and wept at the bank. She stayed there and wept and did not eat or drink or sleep until she finally died. Her soul now walks the rivers edge weeping and looking for her precious sons.

Lover's Lane

A girl and her boyfriend, looking for a little privacy, decide to park their car in the woods so they could make out. When they were done, the boy got out to go to the bathroom and the girl waited for him in the safety of the car.

After waiting five minutes she became nervous and got out of the car to look for him. Suddenly, she sees a man in the shadows. Scared, she gets back in the car to drive away, when she hears a very faint squeak... squeak... squeak...

This continued a few seconds until the girl decided she had no choice but to drive off. She hit the gas as hard as possible but couldn't go anywhere, because someone had tied a rope from the bumper of the car to a nearby tree.

Well, the girl slams on the gas again and then hears a loud scream. She gets out of the car and realizes that her boyfriend is hanging from the tree. The squeaky noises were his shoes slightly scraping across the top of the car!!! for the new and improved version of this site, a searchable database being updated constantly by users. a forum, galleries, polls and more.

The Hook

Two teenage lovers were parked at a local "Make-out" spot when the music on the radio was interrupted by a Special Bulletin. A dangerous Lunatic had escaped from the nearby Insane Asylum, he could be identified by the Hook he had in place of his right hand. The girl insisted she be taken home immediately. When they arrived at her house, the frustrated boy marched over to open her door for her, and hanging from the handle was a bloody hook.

The Nut & the Nuts

A young woman was driving alone one night near the local Insane Asylum when she heard on the radio that a dangerous Lunatic had escaped. Within minutes she heard a pop and felt one of her tires go flat. She built up her nerve and got out and began to change the tire. Just as she slid the spare on, she noticed a man in a plain white uniform staring at her from the bushes. Startled, she dropped the lugnuts and heard them scatter on the ground, as she vainly searched in the darkness for the scattered lug-nuts she heard the man slowly approaching. Terrified, she asked herself in a trembling voice, "What am I going to do now?" and the Lunatic replied "Why don't you take one nut from each of the other wheels and put them on the spare?" She did, and was soon on her way.

The Roommate's Death

A young girl was lying in her room alone one night, her roommate had warned her she'd be out late, when she heard a gurgling, groan coming toward the room. Frightened, she jumped in the closet and locked the door. The sound came closer until it was obvious it was right outside the door, and then whatever it was began to scratch on the door. It didn't stop for what seemed like a long time, and even after the trembling girl was afraid to move, and eventually fell asleep curled up in the closet. The next morning she opened the door to find her roommate lying dead, her throat cut and her fingers and nails bloody from scratching the door for help.

Mama Cass and Her Ham Sandwich

"Mama" Cass Elliot's death has been reported over the years as having been caused by "choking on a sandwich while in bed and from inhaling her own vomit." The true cause of death, a heart attack, was not determined until an autopsy was performed a week later, but by that time it was too late. Another of rocks was born. The proof is in the piggy.

At 5'5" and 238 lbs., Mama Cass was twice the normal weight for a woman her age and height. The effects of long-term obesity, drug abuse and crash diets had weakened her heart to the point of failure. Because she was a large woman, and there was a sandwich on the nightstand when her body was found, an irreversible connection was made. That it was a ham sandwich (an obvious commentary on her weight) was added after the fact. However, no traces of were found blocking her trachea, and there was never any indication that played a role in her death.

The Ultimate Urban Legends

3 Men and a Baby Ghost

There is a scene in the movie Three Men and a Baby where you can see the ghostly figure of a small boy who was killed in the house where the scene was filmed. There are also tales of other ghostly objects being seen throughout the movie, most notably a rifle pointing at the head of the "ghost boy".

That is the legend. Here are the facts. The scene in question was not shot in a house, but on a soundstage in a studio. The "ghost boy" is in fact a life-sized cardboard cut-out of Ted Danson (who stars in the film), which had been left in the background, presumably accidentally, by a crew member. This cut-out is seen in full view in another scene in the movie.

There is no ghost boy. No boy ever died on the set, and no one involved with the movie was ever sued by the mythical parents of said ghost boy.

Mercritis

In Mississippi there is a story about a disease called Mercritis that slipped over from Europe. Men who catch it emit an odour that when inhaled by a beautiful woman, will make her homicidal.

There was a riot in the 1950's during a Mercritis outbreak that swept the southern states and was covered up by the community.

Growing up in the south, people were always saying 'Oh yeah, it's true, my cousin's friend had it...etc., etc., etc.."

Our research online produced no actual references to this condition, but did produce rumour, speculation, and self promotion. Here is an account we found describing the "condition."

"Mercritis Condition (MC) typically leads its victim down a road of trouble, into a life of alienation, interspersed with moments of great violence. Mercritis effects less than

1/10,000,000 of the general population. It strikes males of any age and is only contracted, as far as we know, from the oral consumption of mass amounts of certain types of paint. One of the reasons Mercritis is rare is that paint consumption leads to massive organ failure and many who may have a grim chance of developing the rare disease die before MC manifests. The prevailing theory holds that the victim's skin, fed by secretions resident in the liver and kidneys, releases a mild odour that has an effect on women. Haruki Ryu, formerly of the Yokohama Crier and the only author of a book on the subject (loosely translated) "Mercritis, I run", 1968, Shyu Nai Press, Limited) said in a phone, "the scent seems to effect all women on a hormonal level that appears to alter them emotionally. Irritability and hostility tend to inhabit the milder range of reactivity. That pretty women are so hyper- activated by victims of MC has brought us to speculate on a possible relationship between hormonal activity and beauty. Hyper-activated reactions are called MAR (Mercritis Activated Rage) episodes. Why a woman with no history or pattern of violence would react so strongly to a man with MC has not been adequately studied. In a way, we're all guessing, but in defence of my book, I operate from an educated guess."

The Crash

A young girl had decided to sneak out of the house to go to a party her protective parents wouldn't allow her to go to. While she was there she hooked up with a guy she liked and they went to a local make-out spot. The guy was drinking heavily and when he got too demanding she insisted on him taking her back to the party. On the way back they crashed into another vehicle. When the girl awoke in the hospital she knew she was dying, she was told that they guy she'd been with had died in the accident and so had the couple in the other car. She begged a nurse to tell her parents that she was very sorry she'd disobeyed them, the nurse just looked at her. After the girl died another nurse asked why she hadn't said anything with the teen had asked her to give the message to her parents. The nurse said, "I didn't know what to say, the people in the other car were her parents." - Jezuz

The Fast Train

A not particularly bright man takes a high speed train to get home from a business meeting on the other side of the state. While riding, he looks out the train window to admire the beautiful country side. A woman from behind yells "Look out!" so the man leans farther out the window to see. A loud "whack" sounded as the man's head was chopped off be a passing tree. - Bonkers

The Shadow Cross

An atheist who was training for the Olympics had been given special pool privileges at the university he was attending. Late one night he was considering the arguments a religious friend had been confronting him with as he climbed the high-dive for a little late-night practice. He stood on the board and prepared for a backward flip when he noticed the shadow he was casting on the wall formed a perfect cross in the partially-lit room. Shaken, he sat down on the board to think. As he sat there a maintenance worker came into the pool area and turned on the rest of lights and the diver saw that the pool had been drained for maintenance.

The Stuck Santa

One Christmas Eve a man dressed up as Santa Claus tried to go down his chimney to surprise his young. It wasn't until he started to stink that they realize he'd gotten stuck and been cooked. -Also told as he broke his neck, or got stuck and died from smoke inhalation.

The Merry Go Round

The man who owned the Merry Go Round decided to close it down because he didn't have enough customers coming to the amusement park where he held the ride. Instead of buying the owner out, the park simply boarded up the carousel and this part of the park became very much abandoned for a number of years. 10 years after the ride was closed the original owners daughter thought it was a shame to have the beautiful Merry Go Round boarded up and forgotten in this manner. She and her boyfriend decided to bring some publicity to the park and the ride and reopen the carousel. The boyfriend was going to ride the Merry Go Round for 72 hours straight. The boards were removed, the lights and music turned on and the press had arrived. He made a big show of patting his chosen horse on the nose and mounting the horse he would be riding for the next 72 hours. Surprisingly he was on the ride for less then 10 minutes, when he started complaining that the horse bit him. No one believed him and his girlfriend became very upset, saying that he was letting her down and backing out of the promise he had made. About 5 minutes later, he fell off the horse to the floor of the ride. They shut off the ride and ran to investigate. They found that he had died. The upset girlfriend Military began shaking in disbelief and backed up into the horse he was riding which immediately began to hiss violently. They looked into the horse's mouth and saw that a poisonous snake was hiding inside.

Two Way Mirror

HOW TO DETECT A 2-WAY MIRROR

When we visit toilets, bathrooms, hotel rooms, changing rooms, etc., how many of you know for sure that the seemingly ordinary mirror hanging on the wall is a real mirror, or actually a 2-way mirror (i.e., they can see you, but you can't see them)? There have been many cases of people installing 2-way in female changing rooms. It is very difficult to positively identify the surface by just looking at it. So, how do we determine with any amount of certainty what type of mirror we are looking at? Just conduct this simple test:

Place the tip of your fingernail against the reflective surface and if there is a GAP between your fingernail and the image of the nail, then it is a GENUINE mirror. However, if your fingernail DIRECTLY TOUCHES the image of your nail, then BEWARE, FOR IT IS A 2-WAY MIRROR! So remember, every time you see a mirror, do the "fingernail test." It doesn't cost you anything. It is simple to do, and it might save you from getting "visually raped"! Military

The Hoboken Monkey Man

The Ultimate Urban Legends

My dad loved telling me about various places in New Jersey. One that I especially liked was the one about the Hoboken Monkeyman.

As legend goes, in the early 1980's there supposedly was a Monkeylike beast roaming the streets of Hoboken and terrorizing .Buy apparel and gifts featuring this image of the The police department received so many "Hoboken Monkey Man"! Panicked phone calls that they had to set up a task force to catch him. But they couldn't catch him! On some nights people still say that they see him walking down Washington Street... ...but maybe that's after they had a hard night of drinking?

Termite Mulch Warning Mulch Warning

If you use mulch around your house be very careful about buying mulch this year. After the Hurricane in New Orleans many trees were blown over. These trees were then turned into mulch and the state is trying to get rid of tons and tons of this mulch to any state or company who will come and haul it away. So it will be showing up in Home Depot and Lowes at dirt cheap prices with one huge problem; Formosan Termites will be the bonus in many of those bags. New Orleans is one of the few areas in the country were the Formosan Termites has gotten a stronghold and most of the trees blown down were already badly infested with those termites. Now we may have the worst case of transporting a problem to all parts of the country that we have ever had. These termites can eat a house in no time at all and there apparently is no good control against them, so tell your friends that own homes to avoid cheap mulch and know were it came from.

Neck Scarf

There once was a girl who always wore a scarf around here neck no matter what time of year it was. One day while out on a date with her boyfriend, he said to her "Take off your scarf." She replied, "No, I will take it off when the time is right."

Years went by and the couple became engaged to be married. On their wedding night, her new husband again said to her,

"We are married now so you can take off your scarf." Again she said, "No, I will take it off when the time is right."

More time passed and the young couple grew old together. The old woman lay on her death bed and addressed her weeping husband kneeling by her side. "I'm so sorry to keep this secret from you for so long. Take off my scarf and you'll see why I've always had it on."

Her husband took the end of the scarf in his hand and slowly removed it from her neck. Horrified, he watched his wife's head roll off the bed and across the floor. She'd been wearing the scarf to keep her head on! Angelica Elgin from MN

Hypodermic Needles on Gas Pumps, Pay Phones, etc.

My name is Captain Abraham Sands of the Jacksonville, Florida Police Department. I have been asked by state and local authorities to write this email in order to get the word out to car drivers of a very dangerous prank that is occurring in numerous states.

Some person or persons have been affixing hypodermic needles to the underside of gas pump handles. These needles appear to be infected with HIV positive blood. In the Jacksonville area alone there have been 17 cases of people being stuck by these needles over the past five months.

We have verified reports of at least 12 others in various states around the country. It is believed that these may be copycat incidents due to someone reading about the crimes or seeing them reported on the television. At this point no one has been arrested and catching the perpetrator(s) has become our top priority.

Shockingly, of the 17 people who where stuck, eight have tested HIV positive and because of the nature of the disease, the others could test Military positive in a couple years.

Evidently the consumers go to fill their car with gas, and when picking up the pump handle get stuck with the infected needle. IT IS IMPERATIVE TO CAREFULLY CHECK THE

HANDLE of the gas pump each time you use one. LOOK AT
EVERY SURFACE YOUR HAND MAY TOUCH,
INCLUDING UNDER THE HANDLE.

If you do find a needle affixed to one, immediately contact
your local police department so they can collect the evidence.

Never Ending Road

In Corona, California there once was a road known by most
locals as the Never Ending Road .Specifically, the roads true
name was Lester Road. Now, over twenty years later, the
landscape of Corona has changed, and the Never Ending Road
is no more. However, years ago, Lester Road was an unlit road
that people claimed became a never ending road when driven
at night. The people who made such a drive were never seen
from again.

The legend became so well-known that people refused to even
drive Lester Road during the day. One night, like many teens
my age, I drove up Lester Road, but only a short distance, and
in my headlights it did look like it went on forever.
Frightened, I quickly turned around, because if I continued up
the road, I may never return again. Military Perpetuation of
the legend convinced local law enforcement to investigate.
Lester Road took a sharp left turn at its end, and there were no
guard rails. Beyond the curve lay a canyon, and on the other
side of the canyon was another road that lined up so well with
Lester Road that when viewed from the correct angle,
especially at night, the canyon vanished from sight, and the
road seemed to continue on up and over the hill on the other
side of the canyon. Upon investigation of the canyon, dozens
of were found, fallen to their doom, with the decomposing
bodies of the victims still strapped to their seats.

At around 10 pm one stormy night, the last bus form
Nottingham to Mansfield stopped outside Newsted Abby, a
widely known haunted place in the UK. It was raining heavily
and the driver almost missed the man who was waiting at the
stop as this was the first time in many years a person had been
picked up at this stage of the route. The man got on the bus
and walked up to the top deck without saying a word.

The driver woke the conductor who had fallen asleep to go serve the man with a Military ticket. The groggy man noticed the bad weather outside and a lack of wet foot prints on the bus floor he asked the driver if he was joking. After a short disagreement on the matter, the conductor went up to find the man, only to discover the top deck was empty. The annoyed conductor stormed down to tell the driver that he was not in the mood for jokes. The driver argued that he was telling the truth, and the argument got so intense that the driver stopped the bus. As he turned to face the conductor and continue the heated discussion, the man came down the stairs and began to walk towards them.

"I told you," the driver said to the conductor, then he turned his attention to the man and said "Sorry mate, but this isn't the bus stop." The man continued past them and stood at the door without saying a word. The driver, once again, tried to inform the silent passenger that this was not a bus stop, but the man just stood at the door and didn't speak. The conductor began to realize that something creepy was happening and reached over to the driver's controls to open the door.

The quiet man walked out into the rain and as he disappeared into the night, just then the driver and conductor realized that somehow they were once again outside Newsted Abby.

Man With No Face

One of the most famous intravenous drugs for generating stories about bizarre behaviour was phencyclidine: "angel dust," or "PCP." Although little is heard anymore about angel dust, it was well known for its ability to both addle and confer superhuman powers upon its abusers, or so the stories went. Tales of "some guy who was dusted" going berserk and beating up six cops before fifteen more managed to subdue him abounded. In my work in the [New York General Hospital], I witnessed some exceedingly strange dust-induced behaviour, including one patient who'd done the most bizarre thing to himself I'd ever seen or heard of in Military my life.

This man smoked dust one day and surprised his friends by politely excusing himself to the bathroom, bringing along his two Doberman pinschers. In the bathroom he opened the medicine cabinet, removed a straightedge razor, cut off his own facial features one by one, and fed them to his dogs. He emerged from the bathroom with no ears, nose, eyelids, lips, or cheeks, and two happy-looking dogs.

His friends, now fairly distraught, brought him to the NYG emergency room, where the plastic and head and neck surgeons pissed in their pants with excitement. They took him straight to the operating room. Jokes emerged immediately. The man lost face, the surgeons tried to save face, etc., etc.

In order to create a new face for this unfortunate patient, the surgeons did a "pectoral flap," a fascinating procedure in which the pectoral (chest) muscle is removed and reimplanted at another site on a patient's body. The surgeon's don't remove the muscle completely, but leave intact his main artery and vein. The muscle is then "flapped" to the spot where it's needed, presumably a hole that is too deep to be filled by mere skin grafting, and sewn in place. Eventually, it grows a new blood supply at the transplant site and the surgeons remove the original artery and vein. The man with no face had two pectoral flaps done, one from each side of his chest to each side of his face. Once the muscles were well established in their new locations the surgeons took him back to the OR about two hundred times to cut and shape and revise the graft to create a new face for him.

I know the story of the man with no face is true because I saw him walking down the hall a few weeks after he was admitted. He was wearing a surgical hood turned back in front, with two holes cut out for his eyes, like the "elephant man."

No Nursing Home For Me

About 2 years ago my wife and I were on a cruise through the western Mediterranean aboard a Princess liner. At dinner we noticed an elderly lady sitting alone along the rail of the grand stairway in the main dining room. I also noticed that all the staff, ships officers, Military waiters, busboys, etc., all seemed very familiar with this lady. I asked our waiter who the lady was, expecting to be told that she owned the line, but he said he only knew that she had been on board for the last four cruises, back to back.

As we left the dining room one evening I caught her eye and stopped to say hello. We chatted and I said, "I understand you've been on this ship for the last four cruises". She replied, "Yes, that's true." I stated, "I don't understand" and she replied, without a pause, "It's cheaper than a nursing home". So, there will be no nursing home in my future. When I get old and feeble, I am going to get on a Princess Cruise Ship. The average cost for a nursing home is $200 per day. I have checked on reservations at Princess and I can get a long term discount and senior discount price of $135 per day.

That leaves $65 a day for:

1. Gratuities which will only be $10 per day.

2. I will have as many as 10 meals a day if I can waddle to the restaurant, or I can have room service! (which means I can have breakfast in bed every day of the week). 3. Princess has as many as three swimming pools, a workout room, free washers and dryers, and shows every night. 4. They have free toothpaste and razors, and free soap and shampoo.

5. They will even treat you like a customer, not a patient. An extra $5 worth of tips will have the entire staff scrambling to help you.

6. I will get to meet new people every 7 or 14 days.

7. T.V. broken? Light bulb needs changing? Need to have the mattress replaced? No Problem! They will fix everything and apologize for your Additional inconvenience. 8. Clean sheets and towels every day, and you don't even have to ask for them.

9. If you fall in the nursing home and break a hip you are on Medicare; if you fall and break a hip on the Princess ship they will upgrade you to a suite for the rest of your life.

Now hold on for the best! Do you want to see South America, the Panama Canal, Tahiti, Australia, New Zealand, Asia, or name where you want to go? Princess will have a ship ready to go. So don't look for me in a nursing home, just call shore to ship.

And don't forget, when you die, they just dump you over the side at no charge.

WARNING FROM THE STATE POLICE. . USA (Not a joke.)

State police warning for online: Please read this "very carefully", then send it out to all the people online that you know. Something like this is nothing to be taken casually; this is something you DO want to pay attention to.

If a person with the screen-name of Monkeyman935 contacts you, do not reply. DO not talk to this person; do not answer any of his/her instant messages or e-mail. Whoever this person may be, he/she is a suspect for murder in the death of 56 women (so far) contacted through the Internet. Please send this to all the women on your buddy list and ask them to pass this on, as well. This screen-name was seen on Yahoo, AOL, AIM, and Excite so far.

If Tomorrow Starts Without Me

A few weeks ago a woman teacher was killed in an auto accident. She was very, very well liked, so the school systems shut down for her funeral and it was on the news and so on. On the day the workers came back to work, they found this poem in their e-mail that the deceased woman had sent on Friday before she left for home.

IF TOMORROW STARTS WITHOUT ME

And I'm not there to see; if the sun should rise and find your eyes all filled with tears for me;

The Ultimate Urban Legends

I wish so much you wouldn't cry the way you did today, while thinking of the many things, we didn't get to say.

I know how much you love me; As much as I love you. And each time at you think of me, I know you'll miss me too. But when tomorrow starts without me, please try to understand,

That an angel came and called my name, and took me by the hand.

And said my place was ready, in heaven far above, And that I'd have to leave behind, all those I dearly love. But as I turned to walk away, a tear fell from my eye,

For all my life, I'd always thought, I didn't want to die.

I had so much to live for, So much left yet to do. It seemed almost impossible, that I was leaving you. I thought of all the yesterdays, the good ones and the bad, I thought of all the love we shared, and all the fun we had.

If I could relive yesterday, just even for a while, I'd say good-bye and kiss you, and maybe see you smile. But then I fully realized, that this could never be, for emptiness and memories, would take the place of me.

And when I thought of worldly things, I might miss come tomorrow,

I thought of you, and when I did, my heart was filled with sorrow. But when I walked through heaven's gates, I felt so much at home. When God looked down and smiled at me, from His great golden throne,

He said "This is eternity, and all I've promised you."

Today your life on earth is past, but here life starts anew. I promise no tomorrow, but today will always last. And since each day's the same way, there's no longing for the past.

You have been so faithful, so trusting and so true. Though there were times you did some things,

You knew you shouldn't do. But you have been forgiven, and now at last you're free. So won't you come and take my hand, and share my life with me?

So when tomorrow starts without me, don't think we're far apart.

For every time you think of me, I'm right here, in your heart.

Disappearing Pond

In Monmouth County, New Jersey, on 18th Ave in Belmar at one time was the trail that native American men used to return from fishing in the ocean to where their "squaws" were camped at "Squankum" (near Allaire). At the approximate junction of 18th Ave and the present day Allaire Rd there was a large pond.

One evening a large flock of geese landed on the pond. Overnight the pond froze. When the geese took off in the morning they took the ice that was Military attached to them away. There has not been a pond there since.

This story was published in "Outdoor Life" in the 1950's.

Cheating Husband Loses Porsche

A man saw an ad in the paper for an "almost new" Porsche, in excellent condition - price $50. He was certain the printers had made a typographical error, but even at $5,000 it would have been a bargain, so he hurried to the address to look at the car.

A nice-looking woman appeared at the front door. Yes, she had placed the ad.

The price was indeed $50. "The car," she said, "is in the garage. Come and look at it."

The fellow was overwhelmed. It was a beautiful Porsche and, as the ad promised, "nearly new." He asked if he could drive the car around the block. The woman said, "Of course," and went with him. The Porsche drove like a dream. The young man peeled off $50 and handed it over, somewhat sheepishly. The woman gave him the necessary papers, and the car was his. Finally, the new owner couldn't stand it any longer. He had to know why the woman would sell the Porsche at such a ridiculously low price. Her reply was simple:

With a half-smile on her face, she said, "My husband ran off with his secretary a few days ago and left a note instructing me to sell the car and the house, and Military send him the money." Rat Dog

The truck driver's wife works in Boston on the docks where this little white dog comes around at noon and everyone feeds it a little something from their lunch. The wife went home and asked her husband if he would mind if she got a dog. She told him about the stray that everyone has been feeding. He said that he didn't think she wanted a dog. She said it would be nice company since he was away from home a lot, so he agreed.

The next time she went to work, she saw the little stray as usual. Everyone gave Military him something to eat and she coaxed the dog into her car and brought him home. She washed, cleaned and bathed him, and the dog slept with her in their bed that night and the next.

The next day she came home from work and found the dog had eaten her beloved cat! Horrified, she was confronted with the gruesome sight of a large spot of blood on the floor and all that remained was her cat's skull sitting nearby. The panicked woman called the veterinarian who told her to bring the dog right in. He could not do anything for the cat, but the bones from the cat could do injury to the dog.

She brought the dog in to see the vet and was in the waiting room when one of the vet techs nervously asked her to step into one of the rooms immediately! When she got in the room the vet asked her where she got the dog and she told her it was a stray she found where she works near the docks in Boston.

The vet told her the animal needed to be put down immediately. The stray she had taken in was not a dog, but a 40-pound Cambodian rat that came in from one of the ships in the harbour. The rat was so big that it looked liked a small dog with a little snub tail.

Rhubarb Rover

It starts one night in the middle of the moors at Exmoor, in Devon, UK, at around about 11pm in the winter of 1982. An elderly lady was walking her dog, as she normally did, when she heard a haunting grumbling noise coming from somewhere in the darkness in front of her. (I don't know whether you're familiar with moors: they are usually quite foggy and murky, with no light to be seen except for the glow of the moon) This worried her somewhat, and with that she decided to turn and walk rapidly toward the direction of her home. After about 20 minutes, she arrived at her doorstep, with her dog, to find her front door locked. She fumbled nervously for her keys and unlocked the door, and desperately entered the house.

The dog, however refused to go in, instead choosing to roll in the mud nearby to her husband's prized rhubarb plant.

To this day, the rhubarb still looks fine, and the dog never did it again, even when coaxed. Subsequently, it had a puppy called Custard that was only born after her husband died.

Killing Saviour

A girl and her fiends were walking home from a party. They heard a rustling noise during their walk, but they forgot about it instantly.

Her friends lived in another neighbourhood, so the girl was soon walking home by herself. She heard the noise again, and then she heard footsteps approaching so she started to jog. The following footsteps quickened with hers and sounded like they were jogging behind her. She became panicked started to run and so did whoever was following her. The girl ran into the road without looking and she was immediately hit and run over by a speeding truck. The young woman died instantly.

The stalker who was following the girl witnessed the driver of the truck hit her prey. This Good Samaritan driver saw the girl being followed and began to cry and call 911 on her cell phone. When the girl ran out into the street, the distracted driver struck and killed the girl she was trying to save.

Shades of Death Road

Legend has it, that many years ago, a car of teenagers were driving down a country road in Hacketsttown after the prom. Due to the windy nature of the path, and slippery conditions, the car crashed into a ditch and a girl, still in her prom dress, died. To this day, you can still see her wandering the curve that she was murdered on wearing her dress.

The road is actually named, "Shades of Death Road" and is located towards Great Meadows by Jenny Jump State Park and Ghost Lake (A highly haunted area). The road is very windy and tales tells that if you, as an unsuspecting teenager, drive too fast down Shades of Death Road, the ghost of the dead girl will present herself to you, there by forcing you into a fiery death as well - perhaps a warning to others?

Part of the story also includes this tid bit: Every section of the road that contains a reflective guardrail is where someone has died.

The Sloppy Joe

A butcher named Joe owned a diner with his wife, whom he loved dearly. One evening Joe came home to find his wife having sex with his best friend. Joe went crazy finding out about their affair this way. He yelled and screamed and during their heated argument, Joe killed them both. He disposed of the bodies by chopping them up and sending them piece by piece through his meat grinder.

The next day, Joe called his dearly departed wife's parents and the parents of his ex best friend and invited them to dinner at

90

the diner. There he told them that the two cheaters had run off together and left him a note telling him she wanted a divorce and that she and his friend were to be married.

Joe served the uncomfortable and confused parents their dinner. Ground meat in Military a special sauce on a bun. The meat had a unique flavour, one the family had never tasted before. His mother-in-law said "This is delicious, but its kind of sloppy Joe."

Since then, Joe started selling Sloppy Joes at his diner.

It's also the reason that sloppy joes are also called "Man-Wich". The meat in the sandwich was made from the man and the "witch" who committed adultery and the horrible act of betrayal against the butcher.

Ticket Frenzy

This could also be under the category because that's how it came to me.

BEWARE! Jersey will launch a 30 day speeding ticket frenzy. The state estimates that 9 million dollars will be generated in speeding tickets. 1 million will go to pay state troopers over time. There will 50 state troopers on duty at all times patrolling the 9 main intersections and highways.

Sunbathing Spiders

A young woman was sunbathing on the beach and was just about to drop off to sleep, when she felt an insect running along her jawbone and then down her neck. She brushed it away, and thought nothing more of it.

After about a week, she noticed what she thought was a pimple growing and growing. The skin was inflamed and it looked like a blister. Then, one day, she was blow-drying her hair and hit the inflamed spot with her hair dryer. The blistered skin broke open and hundreds of tiny white baby spiders and pus came pouring out of the wound! It seems that while she was sunbathing, her pores had enlarged enough that a mama spider could deposit her egg sac in one. They incubated under her skin until she smacked herself in the jaw with the hair dryer! Two-Striped Telamonia

A spider bite...please read........... And you thought the brown recluse was bad!!!

Three women in North Florida, turned up at hospitals over a 5-day period, all with the same symptoms. Fever, chills, and vomiting, followed by muscular collapse, paralysis, and finally, death. There were no outward signs of trauma. Autopsy results showed toxicity in the blood. These women did not know each other, and seemed to have nothing in common.

It was discovered, however, that they had all visited the same Restaurant (Olive Garden) within days of their deaths. The health department descended on the restaurant, shutting it down. The, water, and air conditioning were all inspected and tested, to no avail.

The big break came when a waitress at the restaurant was rushed to the hospital with similar symptoms. She told doctors that she had been on vacation, and had only went to the restaurant to pick up her check. She did not eat or drink while she was there, but had used the restroom. That is Military when one toxicologist, remembering an article he had read, drove out to the restaurant, went into the restroom, and lifted the toilet seat.

Under the seat, out of normal view, was a small spider. The spider was captured and brought back to the lab, where it was determined to be the Two-Striped Telamonia (Telamonia dimidiata), so named because of its reddened flesh colour. This spider's venom is extremely toxic, but can take several days to take effect. They live in cold, dark, damp climates, and toilet rims provide just the right atmosphere. Several days later a lawyer from Jacksonville showed up at a hospital emergency room. Before his death, he told the doctor, that he had been away on business, had taken a flight from Indonesia, changing planes in Singapore, before returning home. He did not visit

(Olive Garden), while there. He did, as did all of the other victims, have what was determined to be a puncture wound, on his right buttock. Investigators discovered that the flight he was on had originated in India. The Civilian Aeronautics Board (CAB) ordered an immediate inspection of the toilets of all flights from India, and discovered the Two-Striped Telamonia (Telamonia dimidiata) spider's nests on 4 different planes!

It is now believed that these spiders can be anywhere in the country. So please, before you use a public toilet, lift the seat to check for spiders. It can save your life! And please pass this on to everyone you care about.

Thump, Thump, Drag...

Ashley, a 16 year old girl, was babysitting 2 little boys. Their parents weren't supposed to come home until very late, so she put them to bed and sat downstairs in the living room to watch some TV. She was flipping channels and came to the evening news. The Anchor-woman reported a warning for her area. She said that a mental patient had escaped from a nearby facility and was on the run from the local authorities. Ashley flipped the channel again to find an old movie she hadn't seen in a while, but always enjoyed. By the end of the film, she had forgotten about the news report. Upstairs one of the boys woke up. He thought he heard a noise coming from the hallway. Thump, thump, draaaag....

The child thought that Ashley must be watching TV, the sound must have been from the program she was watching.

The boy heard the sound again and woke his brother. Together, they listened at the door to the bedroom and the sound kept coming thump, thump, Military draaaag...thump, thump, drag....

The sound stopped but the boys were still nervous about leaving the safety of their bedroom. They got back into bed and stayed under the covers until their parents got home.

When their parents came in the house they were struck by a gruesome sight. Ashley was laying halfway up the stairs with a trail of blood behind her. Her arms were cut off at the elbows and she'd been climbing the stairs on the bloody stumps of her arms, pulling her badly injured body along to protect the before she died of blood loss.

Ashley's attacker was never found!

Movie Tickets

A man and his wife went out for the night with friends who picked them up at their house. They left their new Mercedes Benz parked outside. When they came home they realized that their new car had disappeared.

They called the police to report the theft and searched fruitlessly for the rest of the night. Devastated by their loss, they went home and went to sleep.

The next morning, they woke up to see their car parked outside their home, just the way they left it the night before. A note was on the windshield explaining that a man and his wife needed it so they could drive to the local hospital. The grateful and influential man left tickets for the couple to go to a movie premier in the city the next night.

The couple was thrilled to have their car back and excited to go to the premier. They dressed up and attend the movie the next night. When they got home from the event they found that their home had been robbed and all of their belongings were gone. All they had left was the car they thought they lost the night before.

The shocked couple searched the house and found a note saying: HOPE YOU ENJOYED THE MOVIE! Bobby Lee from WV and Ashley from FL Turkey Baby

A newlywed couple had their first baby. Because Annie (the mom), was afraid to leave the baby alone with anyone, the once social couple, found themselves spending their nights at home. Finally, when the baby was about 5 months old, Annie's husband Jack decided to hire a babysitter to watch the child while the couple went to a friend's birthday party.

Once the couple had left, the babysitter invited her boyfriend over to Annie and Jack's house to party. He brought her some booze and together they drank liquor and tried LSD, something they had never done before. When Annie called home to check on the baby, the babysitter told her about the pretty colours and the turkey that she was cooking in the oven.

Annie got very upset and went to find her husband so they could rush home and see what was going on. When they got to their house, Jack ran upstairs to get the baby, and Annie stayed with the babysitter to try and make sense of what she had said earlier on the phone. Jack came running down the stairs in a panic asking over an over again "Where's the baby? Where's the baby?" Suddenly, both Jack and Annie smelled something burning. They ran to the kitchen, looked in the oven and found their beautifully burnt baby.

The Ghostly Violin

In Houston, Texas there was a security guard, janitor, or some other poor guy who worked the night shift in the public library. He was apparently well-liked by everyone who used the facility and was made unusual by the fact that he played the violin, loved to do so with an unending passion and often engaged in his musical pursuit during his down time, much to the delight of all who heard him.

When the good fellow eventually died, apparently of natural causes, it was (and may still be) reported that his violin could still be heard around the library during the quiet of the evening.

Mall Warning

To the men: warn your loved ones!

To the women: remember this! About a month ago there was a woman standing by the Mega Mall entrance passing out flyers to all the women going in. The woman had written the flyer herself to tell about an experience she had, so that she might warn other women.

The previous day, this woman had finished shopping, went out to her car and discovered that she had a flat. She got the jack out of the trunk and began to change the flat. A nice man dressed in business suit and carrying a briefcase walked up to her and said, "I notice you are changing a flat tire. Would you like me to take care of it for you?" The woman was grateful for his offer and accepted his help. They chatted amiably while the man changed the flat, and then put the flat tire and the jack in the trunk, shut it and dusted his hands off.

The woman thanked him profusely, and as she was about to get in her car, when the man told her that he left his car around on the other side of the mall, and asked if she would mind giving him a lift to his car.

She was a little surprised and asked him why his car was on other side. Military He explained that he had seen an old friend in the mall that he hadn't seen for some time and they had a bite to eat and visited for a while; he got turned around in the mall and left through the wrong exit, and now he was running late and his car was clear around on the other side of the mall.

The woman hated to tell him "no" because he had just rescued her from having to change her flat tire all by herself, but she felt uneasy.

Then she remembered seeing the man put his briefcase in her trunk before shutting it and before he asked her for a ride to his car.

She told him that she'd be happy to drive him to his car, but she just remembered one last thing she needed to buy. She said she would only be few minutes; he could sit down in her car and wait for her; she would be as quick as she could be.

She hurried into the mall, and told a security guard what had happened; the guard came out to her car with her, but the man had left.

The Ultimate Urban Legends

They opened the trunk, took out his locked briefcase and took it down to the police station. The police opened it (ostensibly to look for ID so they could return it to the man). What they found was rope, duct tape and knives.

When the police checked her "flat" tire, there was nothing wrong with it; the air had simply been let out. It was obvious what the man's motive was, and obvious that he had carefully thought it out in advance.

The woman was blessed to have escaped harm. How much worse it would have been had she waited in the car while the man fixed the tire, or if she had a baby strapped into a car seat. Or if she'd gone against her judgment and given him a lift.

A candle is not dimmed by lighting another candle. I was going to send this to the ladies only; but guys, if you love your mothers, wives, sisters, daughters, etc., you may want to pass it on to them, as well.

Send this to any woman you know that may need to be reminded that the world we live in has a lot of crazies in it....

PLEASE BE SAFE AND NOT SORRY!

Which Tire?

Two students decide to go skiing for the weekend, and are having such a good time they decide to blow off the exam that they have scheduled for Monday morning in order to get some final runs in before they head back to school. They decide to tell the professor that they got a flat tire and therefore deserve to take the exam at a rescheduled time.

Hearing the story, said professor agrees that it really was just bad luck, and of course they can take the exam later. At the appointed time, the professor greets them and places them in two separate rooms to take the exam.

The few questions on the first page are worth a minor 10% of the overall grade, and are quite easy. Each student grows progressively confident as they take the test, sure that they have gotten away with fooling the professor. However, when they turn to the second page they discover that they really haven't.

The only question on the page, worth 90% of the exam, reads: "Which tire?" Heeeeeeelp Meeeeee! One dark and stormy night a woman was listening to her extensive Cliff Richard CD collection when she heard a strange sound. It sent a chill down her spine as she heard a low humming and buzzing noise emanating from under her bed. She bent down nervously and noticed, to her utter horror, that her Walkman had mysteriously turned itself on and was playing an ominous tune...........backwards.

She quickly snatched the tape player from under her bed and as she did so, she very faintly heard the following words: "Hhhhheeeeeelp meeeeeeee!" In terror she ripped the batteries out of the machine, but it carried on with its haunting plea.

Petrified, she ran to her neighbour's house and was relieved to find her awake. The neighbour managed to calm her down with some kind words and a stiff drink. She explained to the neighbour the disturbing night's events, and then they both plucked up the courage to go back to her house to find out what on earth was happening. Upon their return, the Walkman had stopped, but the words "Help Me!" were written on the floor.

The next day the newspaper headline screamed "Sir Cliff Killed in Car Crash!" He was reportedly heard screaming "help me" by witnesses as his car skated over the icy cliff......How scary is that?

The Wizard of Oz

A friend told me that in one scene of the Wizard of Oz you can see someone 'hang' themselves from a tree in the background. There's no place like home... Well, the "dead person hanging in the background" rumour is popular, but untrue. What the "hanging person" actually it is a film crew person who got caught in the shot and quickly ran off the set.

98

It's kinda hard to see, but it never did get cut out. I guess the hanging person legend has too much flare to die down.

9-11

There were no taxis around the World Trade Center at the time of the attack.

The next terrorist attacks will stem from 7-11 stores on the date 7/11.

People "in the know" have been warned not to drink Coca-Cola after June 1st.

The Baby on the Roof

A young couple were driving down the highway one day and decided it was time to switch drivers. As they changed places they left their infant child on the roof of the car and drove off.

God Took Them

When a little girl's cat had kittens they disappeared after a couple of days, when she asked her mother what happened to them and her mother said "God took them." Months later the cat again had a litter of kittens. Her mother sent her out to run some errands, but before she left she wanted to play with the kittens again. She heard her father coming carrying a bucket and hid from him. She watched while her father put the kittens in a sack and drowned them in the bucket. Later the girl again asked her mother what happened to the kittens. Her mother said "God took them." Several days later the mother asked the girl to watch her brother in the bath tub while she answered the phone. The mother screamed when she came into the bathroom after a few minutes. The girl told her "God took him."

-Serves 'em right. Anyone too stupid to take care of pets responsibly shouldn't breed .

Three Dead Kids

The Ultimate Urban Legends

A woman was giving her daughter a bath while her 3 year old son was supposed to be watching her infant. The boy found the soft spot on the baby's head and pushed, and pressed his finger into the child's brain and killed it. Horrified the boy ran out of the house and into the street where he was hit by an oncoming truck. The woman ran outside to see what was going on, after her hysterical reaction she discovered that the daughter had drowned in the bathtub.

The Cement Cadillac

A cement-truck driver had an order to deliver a load of wet cement just around the block from his house one day and he decided to stop by and have coffee with his beautiful wife. When he got there he saw a shiny new Cadillac parked in his spot. Feeling a little suspicious he peeked in the window and saw her having coffee with some handsome rich guy. Without a pause he got in his truck and filled the caddy with his leftover cement. His wife ran out of the house and asked him why he'd just destroyed the new car she'd just had delivered for him.

Cruise Control

An elderly couple had just purchased a brand-new RV and headed off across the country. The old man explained to his wife that the salesman had showed him how to use the vehicle's "auto-pilot", he said that all he had to do was press the button marked "cruise" and relax. So the old man set his cruise control and went in the back for a nap. He had just gotten comfortable when the RV went off the cliff.

The Deal

There's a little old lady whose son bought himself a brand new car before being sent to Vietnam. He gets killed and the car sits in her garage covered up for the next twenty years until she finally brings herself to sell it. She places an ad in the local paper selling the car for the same amount her son paid for it, $2000. When a potential buyer shows up to look at it he discovers it is a 1963 Corvette Stingray in mint condition. -

No Radio

A man who was tired of having his vehicles broken into specifically asked for no radio when he bought his new car. He put a sign in the windshield that said in large letters: "NO RADIO". One day he returned to it to find the windshield broken anyway. Beside his sign he found a note that read: "Just checking."

- Sometimes the note says "No Windshield" or "Get one".

The Rattle

A man purchased a brand new luxury sedan, loaded with extras and very expensive. The car was perfect except for a persistent, annoying rattle. He took the car back to the dealer and had every part of it checked and tightened, but the rattle continued. Finally he had the car completely dismantled and inside one of the door panels they found the source of the rattle, it was several nuts and bolts tied to a string with a note attached. The note read: "I GUESS YOU FINALLY FOUND THE RATTLE."

Sell the Car

A man runs off with a little cutie and sends his wife a Dear Jane letter telling him he's not coming back and he wants a divorce. He tells his wife to sell his Porsche and send him half the proceeds. She runs an ad "Porsche for Sale, $20" and sends him his check for $10.

The Smashed VW

A couple had been awakened by the sound of a crash on the edge of their property one night. They looked out and saw two eighteen-wheelers had been in a head on collision and immediately called 911. The policeman told them both drivers had been killed on impact and asked if the trucks could stay there until the investigation was over. The couple agreed. A week later the angry homeowner called the policeman and demanded the wrecks be taken away immediately, when the officer arrived with the tow-truck he understood why. Coming from the crash was to most horrible stench he'd ever encountered. When they pulled the trucks apart they found the cause of the smell, in between the trucks was a VW Beetle, smashed flat with three people inside.

The 10 Kilo Gas Tank

A guy looking for a used SUV finds a Lincoln Navigator at a police auction that was seized from a convicted drug dealer. He buys it, but when he fills the gas tank, it doesn't fill all the way. So he takes the car to a shop and the mechanic disassembles the gas tank and finds 10 kilograms of packaged cocaine at the bottom.

The Unstealable Car

A man's biggest fear was that his new sport scar would be stolen and he went to great lengths to insure that didn't happen. Each night he backed the car carefully into the garage, chained the frame to the floor, set the alarm and locked the garage. One morning he entered the garage and was shocked to discover the car was exactly as he always left it, except it had been turned around! On the seat was a note, it read: "WHEN WE WANT IT, WE'LL COME GET IT."

The Wonder Car

An old lady who'd recently bought a new car returned it to the dealer when after driving over 300 miles the gas tank still read "full". The dealer gave her fifty thousand dollars and her choice of any car on the lot in exchange for the experimental car he'd accidentally sold her.

The Body in the Bed

A man and his wife were vacationing in Las Vegas and as they arrived in their room they found it was filled with an overpowering stench. They called the front desk to complain, and headed for the casinos for some late-night gambling while the problem was taken care of. When they returned to the room, the stench was replaced with the strong smell of chemical cleaners and deodorizers, annoyed but satisfied that it was better than before they went to bed. Early in the morning the smell had returned so strongly that it awakened them, the man called the manager and angrily demanded another room immediately. While his wife packed up their stuff the man ripped the sheets off the bed, where the smell seemed to be coming from. He found that the mattress had been cut open and a well-dressed corpse had been shoved inside. The couple were given a complimentary suite and free passes to the shows.

The Decapitated Motorcyclist

A Man on a motorcycle was passing an eighteen-wheeler carrying sheet metal when one of the sheets shifted and neatly cut off the driver's head. His headless body continued on its path by the semi. The driver saw the headless cyclist and immediately had a heart-attack, and his truck swerved into a bus-stop full of people.

AIDS Mary

A man met a beautiful woman in a singles bar one night and took her home. During the evening she told him that she had been raped a few years ago, but was overcoming her resentment and fear, and was finally able to enjoy sex again. The next morning he awoke to find her already gone, on the bathroom mirror she'd written a message in lipstick. "Welcome to the AIDS club."

The exact wording of the message varies, and often the legend ends with the guy searching for "Mary" hoping to kill her before he himself dies.

The Arm

An unpopular young med. student had been particularly annoying one day and some of her classmates decided to play a trick on her. They snuck into her room after she'd gone to bed and placed an amputated arm into bed with her. The next morning they anxiously awaited her reaction but got none. Eventually they went up to check on her and found her sitting on the bed, moaning and gurgling as she gnawed on the arm.

Bloody Mary

If you stand in front of a mirror in a dark room and chant "Bloody Mary" twelve times starting at the stroke of midnight, the face of a hideous woman will appear in the mirror. It's the spirit of a girl who was born with a disfiguring disease and was killed by a cruel joke gone awry.

This one's a classic. It's told about a thousand different ways, sometimes she scratches, slaps, grabs, kills... The number of chants changes, and what is chanted changes. Some good ones are Black Agnes and Hell Mary. Sometimes she's a witch who was burned at the stake, or an innocent woman accused and burned. The stroke of midnight isn't very common, most the time it merely has to take place at night. I liked it because it makes it more difficult for even the bravest souls not to pause under pressure.

Drinking & Driving

A man got home late from a night out drinking with the boys and staggered inside, his wife heard him and helped him into bed. The next morning she complained about his behavior and how she worried about how he makes it home so drunk. He agreed that he had no memory of the last few hours of his night out, but said he'd never had a problem before. As he pulled out of the garage to go to work, his wife was who had been watching him angrily from the front door screamed when she saw the little girl crushed into the grill of the car.

The Vanishing Hitchhiker

Two guys were driving down the highway one night, when they see a lovely young girl standing by the road shivering. They stop and offer her a ride, and lent her an overcoat. When they dropped her off at her house, they forgot the overcoat as she got out. The next morning they dropped by to get it and see that the girl was ok, her mother told them her only daughter died in a car accident long ago, and showed them her grave as proof. Neatly folded on the grave was the over coat.

This one is told many different ways, in some the girl disappears before they get to her destination, so the guys stop at the house to see what's going on. In some the guys take the girl to the prom before she leaves with the overcoat.

Sometimes she died exactly a year ago to the date, others she died many years ago, but something like this happens every anniversary of her death. Usually she died in the place where the boys picked her up.

The Last Call

One of the Ball Brothers, of the canning jar family, had a great fear of being buried alive. He had a telephone installed in his tomb so he could call out if this happened to him. A few days after he died some of his wife's family got worried because they could only get a busy signal on her phone. Upon entering her home, they found her dead, a look of fright frozen on her face, clutching the phone. When they went to entomb her after the funeral a couple of days later, the phone inside the crypt was off the hook

The Message Under the Stamp

During the war a soldier faithfully wrote his mother every week so she would know he was all right, until one week she didn't get a letter and immediately began to worry. Within a couple of weeks she got a letter from the Army saying that her son had been captured and was being held in a Prisoner-of-War camp, and they assured her that they had no reason to believe the American prisoners were being mistreated in any way. A few weeks later the woman finally received another letter from her son, it read: "Dear Mom, Try not to worry about me, they are treating us well and I'll be released as soon as the war is over. Make sure that little Teddy gets the stamp for his collection. Love you, Joe" The woman was overjoyed to hear the news, but was confused because she had no idea who "little Teddy" was. She decided to steam the stamp from the envelope and have a look. When she did she saw that written on the back of the stamp were the words: "They've cut off my legs".

This may be one of the oldest Urban Legends in existence, it's been circulated during every war since the Civil War. It's ironic since POW camps didn't stamp their mail, being a government institution the mail was metered. It was especially popular during Vietnam, and the part of the body cut off varies.

The Mutilated Bride

A young man and his new bride were honeymooning in Paris when his wife went into a restroom and didn't return. With time the man began to fear the worst and went to the police. The police thought it was most likely the girl simply had second thoughts about the marriage, but they checked it out anyway and found no evidence of foul play. As weeks turned into months the man finally gave up on finding his beautiful wife but his life fell into a shambles he was so filled with grief. Unable to hold a job or go on with his life, he took to wandering the world looking for anything that might ease his pain. Years later in Borneo he came upon a freakshow in an old shabby building, he went in on a whim. In the last filthy cage he saw a twisted, scarred and mutilated woman rocking back and forth and groaning strange animal-like noises. He screamed as he recognized the birthmark on his wife's face.

The Jogger's Billfold

A man was jogging through the park one day when another jogger lightly bumped him and excused himself. A little annoyed, the jogger noticed his wallet was missing. He immediately began chasing the jogging pickpocket and when he caught up he tackled him yelling "Give me that billfold!" The frightened robber obliged and quickly ran off. When the jogger got home his wife asked if he'd stopped at the store. Anxious to tell his story he said he hadn't, but he had a good excuse. Before he finished his wife said: "I know, you left your billfold on the dresser."

The Kind Stranger

An older man who never learned to read or write met a stranger in a bar one afternoon. After about two hours the stranger asked his new friend if he could do him a favor. He wanted him to go to the betting shop across the road and put some money on a horse that was running that afternoon. When the man explained he was illiterate and he couldn't write out a docket the stranger said it was ok as he already had one written out. So the man went to the betting shop and handed in the docket. When the teller took the docket from him and read it she screamed help and dived on the ground. The man was standing at the counter bewildered when all of a sudden five regular customers from the betting shop set upon him and began to beat him. Then the police were called and the man was arrested. When he asked why he was being arrested when he was the one that was attacked and they told him it was for attempted robbery and he could expect a long spell in prison. When he asked how they had come to that conclusion they read the docket to him which read "This is a robbery I have a gun, give me all the money". When he explained about the stranger the police checked it out but no one could be found fitting that description in the bar.

License to Practice

A young woman was waiting for her husband outside a restaurant one evening in a popular Mexican tourist-town when a police officer mistook her for a prostitute. Just as he finished writing up her fine her husband arrived and found out what was going on. The policeman said he was sorry, but they'd have to pay the fine or appear in court. Not wanting alot of trouble, the man simply bought his wife a license to practice prostitution in the city, and they were on their way.

The Perfume Salesman

A woman in a mall parking-lot was approached by someone trying to sell an expensive bottle of perfume for only eight dollars. The salesperson insisted she smell the perfume and she did. A couple hours later she awakened to find her car and all of her belongings had been taken, the bottle had been filled with ether!

The Wheelbarrows

A man who worked in a large factory was stopped on his way out every night as he wheeled out a wheelbarrow full of straw. Each night the suspicious security guard would sift through the straw to make sure the employee wasn't stealing, each night he found nothing but straw. Years later the man was retiring and as he left the guard said that he knew he was stealing something all these years, what was it. The retiree answered "wheelbarrows."

The Killer in the Back Seat

As a woman was getting into her car she noticed a man with a strange look on his face walking quickly toward her. She jumped into the car and drove away, but before long she saw the man was following her in another car. She panicked and drove home as quickly as she could, swerved into the driveway and screamed for her husband. Her husband ran out just as the following man pulled up, jumped from his car and yelled "Lady, there's someone hiding in your back seat!"

The Choking Doberman

A woman came home from shopping to find her Doberman choking on something, she quickly put him in the car and drove him to the vet. The vet told her to go on home while he operated to remove whatever was lodged in the dog's windpipe, and he'd call her when she could pick up her pet. She wasn't home for long when the vet called and told her in an excited voice to get out of the house right now, he'd be by to explain in a few minutes. from her neighbor's window she saw the vet arrive with the police and ran out to see if her dog was alright and what was going on. As the police ran into her house the vet told her what her loving pet had choked on, two human fingers. The police found the escaped Lunatic hiding in the closet nursing his mangled hand.

The Babysitter

A young girl was babysitting some children in a large old house, the children were in bed and she was watching TV when the phone rang. All the voice on the other end did was laugh, she listened for a minute then hung up. A few minutes later it happened again, she was very upset and called the police who told her there was really nothing they could do, but they'd trace the call if it happened again. After she got another call from the laughing voice, she hung up and the police immediately called her and told her to get out of the house immediately, the calls were coming from the upstairs extension, where he'd already murdered the children.

There are many variations of this one, mostly as to what the voice on the phone said or did when he called, it's also been told with two babysitters. The most popular is probably the "Have you checked the Children?" version from the film When a Stranger Calls.

The Licked Hand

A young girl was left alone at home for the first time with only her dog to protect her, she heard a bulletin on the radio about a Dangerous Lunatic that had escaped from a nearby asylum, she immediately locked all the doors and went to bed. A dripping sound from the bathroom made it difficult to fall asleep, she reached down under her bed to make sure her faithful dog was by her side, he replied by licking her hand enthusiastically. The next morning when she woke up and went to the bathroom room, she found her dog hanging from the shower nozzle, blood dripping from his torn throat, on the mirror written in blood were the words: "People can lick, too!"

The Scratching

A young couple were parked under a tree on a dirt road one night. When the time came to go home, the car wouldn't start so the boy told the girl to lock the doors and he'd go for help. As time went by, the girl's nervousness about her situation grew worse, and by the time she started to hear a scraping noise on the top of the car she was terrified. The police found her the next day, as they took her away from the car they told her not to look back, but she did. Her boyfriend was hanging from a tree limb, his feet scraping the roof of the car.

Also: The boyfriend is hanging upside-down from the limb, his fingernails scratching the roof of the car. The girl often ends up in an asylum from the ordeal.

Another Roommate's Death

A young coed was returning from a night out with her friends and she didn't want to disturb her sleeping roommate, so she crept into the room and found her way in the darkness, undressed and slid into bed. The next morning as she awoke and turned to say something to her friend, she saw her mangled body on the blood-soaked bed, and written in her roommate's blood on the wall were the words: "AREN'T YOU GLAD YOU DIDN'T TURN ON THE LIGHT?"

The Cabbage Patch Tragedy

A woman washed cabbage in the washing machine and damaged it badly. Since they were so difficult to come buy she sent it back to the company hoping it could be repaired. A few weeks later she received a death-certificate in the mail, and a bill for the funeral.

Old Almonds

An employee at a nursing home was regularly offered large jars of roasted almonds by one of her very elderly male charges. She appreciated the gifts (she loved almonds), but decided one day to put her foot down - it really wasn't appropriate for a patient to keep giving her gifts. When she approached him about it, he said, "Oh those almonds - they cost me nothing. My family brings me chocolate-coated almonds every time they visit, but I can't chew them, so I just suck the chocolate off them."

The Harvested Children

Homeless children are often "adopted" by a US or European agency where they are put into comas and they're organs are harvested as needed by the wealthy.

The Helpful Children

A woman had just finished grocery-shopping when a group of homeless children offered to help her to her car. After loading her groceries one of the children asked the woman for a tip, grateful she obliged. As she was about to drive off a man ran up to her and told her to go directly to the police station, one of the children had locked himself in the boot to ambush her later with a knife!

The United Kingdom:

Numerous Rolls Royce production plants around the country are actually secret nuclear weapons facilities.

An Oxford/Cambridge philosophy paper once asked only one question; "Is this a question?" The response "No, but this is an answer," won a top First!

Gift Wrappers

As an initiation into a street gang, potential members grab people out of shopping plazas, gift-wrap them from head to toe, then lock them in their trunks.

The Girls' Initiation

To join a gang, prospective female members must have unprotected sex with a HIV+ or AIDs infected member.

The Slashers

As an initiation into a street gang, potential members hide under peoples cars at night, and when the unsuspecting owners start to get in, they slash their ankles and when they fall they steal a shoe.

Spunkball

Gangs of delinquents have been driving around late at night looking for cars with their windows open. At stoplights they yell "Spunkball" and throw a gasoline soaked rag that has been wrapped in aluminum foil in the open window. On the outside of the foil is attached a small fire cracker, with the fuse lit. When the fire cracker explodes, the rag is ignited, causing a large flame that may catch the interior of the car on fire. -

Thread the Needle

Three delinquents were out riding their motorcycles late one night, when the leader decided he would scare the others by riding up ahead of them, turning around and speeding back and driving in between them. After he disappeared from sight, a large semi passed the other bikers. The leader came zipping down the highway and instead of going between his friends bikes, he ran straight between the semi's headlights.

The Tollbooth

Some delinquents pulled up to a tollbooth and asked how much it was, the toll-keeper replied and as he reached out his hand to receive the money, the driver said "What a rip-off! And speaking of rip-offs!" and slapped a handcuff on his wrist. As the car sped off the toll-keeper saw the cuff was tied to a rope that was being pulled out of the back window of the car. Panicking, he tried in vain to remove the cuff before the rope ran out of slack and tore off his arm. Within a few seconds the end of the rope fell harmlessly out the window of the car.

All Aboard

A man was riding the train to an important dinner one night when he realized he'd boarded the wrong train, this was the express that would only slow down at his stop. Desperate not to miss his appointment, when the train neared the town he wanted to go to, stood in the doorway and leaped out as the train passed through the station. He hit the ground running and before he could stop himself a conductor standing in a passing car grabbed his collar and pulled him back onto the train. He said "You're lucky I saw you, don't you know this train doesn't stop here?"

The Electic Slide

A woman came home to find her husband in the kitchen, shaking frantically with what looked like a wire running from his waist towards the electric kettle. Intending to jolt him away from the deadly current she whacked him with a handy plank of wood by the back door, breaking his arm in two places. Until that moment he had been happily listening to his walkman.

Flipping the Bird

A loving son sent his mother a very expensive talking bird that had been specially trained to quote her favorite passages from the bible. When he later asked her what she thought of the bird, she replied "Delicious!"

The Horny Haircut

As an attractive young hairdresser was about to lock up for the evening a sweaty little man knocked and asked her if he could please get a quick trim. She reluctantly obliged and quickly began to trim his hair. As she was finishing up she noticed that under the covering she'd put on him to catch the hair, his hands were moving up and down in his lap. Outraged, she grabbed a large curling iron from the shelf and knocked him unconscious. She called the police and when they arrived they asked what the man had done that had caused her to attack him, she told them, "Just look under the sheet!" The officer pulled the sheet away and said: "Lady, there's no law against a man polishing his eyeglasses!"

The Jogger's Wallet

A man was jogging along one day when another jogger bumped him lightly and excused himself. Already annoyed, the man noticed that his wallet was missing and took off after the jogging pickpocket. He quickly caught up to and tackled him, yelling "Give me that wallet!" The frightened pickpocket gave it up and ran off. When the man returned home his wife asked him if he'd stopped at the store, anxious to tell his tale he said "No, but I have a good excuse!" His wife replied: "I know, you left your wallet on the dresser."

The Mechanic

A woman returns home to discover some hairy legs sticking out from under the car. Thinking her husband has decided to fix the car, she reaches up his leg and gives his privates a bit of a fondle. On entering the kitchen she discovers her husband there as well. Turning very red she rushes back out to the car to find the mechanic unconscious under the car after hitting his head when surprised by her actions.

The Misunderstood Note

A witness at a trial was too embarrassed to repeat the obscenity the defendant had suggested to her, so the judge suggested she write it down, and let the jury read it. The woman did as she was asked, and the note was handed to the jury. The judge told them to each read it carefully and pass it along. The last man in the jury box had fallen asleep, and the young lady next to him woke him and handed it to him. He stared at it in surprise for a couple minutes, then began to fold it up. The judge asked him to please hand the note to the bailiff and the juror replied, "Your honor, this note is a private matter between the lady and myself."

Activist's Rights

Two animal rights protesters were protesting at the cruelty of sending pigs to a slaughterhouse in Bonn. Suddenly the pigs, all two thousand of them, escaped through a broken fence and stampeded, trampling the two hapless protesters to death.

Birds & Rice

You shouldn't throw rice at weddings because when birds eat it it swells in their stomachs and causes hemorrhaging.

A Bug in Her Ear

A young woman was at the beach one day and she thought she felt a bug in her ear, she couldn't find anything, so forgot about it. A few days later she went to see a doctor because of a severe ear ache, he checked her out and decided she must have an earwig- a small bug deep in her inner ear. He said it was too deep to remove, she'd have to wait for it to come out the other side. A few weeks later she found a nasty looking bug on her pillow, put it in a jar and took it to the doctor to see if that was it. He said it was, but the bad news is it was a female and it had laid eggs.

Breath-Sucking Cats

Cats shouldn't be left alone with babies, they'll stick their nose in the baby's nose and suck out its breath.

This is a very old one. Cats will often try to sleep near our faces to enjoy the warmth of our breath, so the cat could suffocate a child by doing so. Most likely this was merely an early explanation for Sudden Infant Death Syndrome.

The Dead Cat in the Package

Two young girls were driving to the mall one day, and accidentally hit and killed a cat. Not wanting any children to see it, they put it in a bag and took it with them so as to dispose of it properly. In the parking lot at the mall, an old woman grabbed the bag and ran off with it. Amused, the girls followed her to see what would happen. They came around the corner and the woman was on the floor clutching her chest and saying "My God, the bag! The bag!" As the ambulance took her away a helpful bystander put the bag in with her since she was so worried about losing it.

Another Dead Cat in a Package

A woman's cat died one day, so she wrapped it in a package and took it with her to dispose of it. She tried to put it in her building's incinerator, but her landlady was there, and pets weren't allowed in the building in the first place. On her way to work she tried to leave it on the bus, but a helpful passenger gave it to her. She tried to leave it in a restaurant, but the waitress chased her down. Even on the subway, there was always a samaritan waiting for a chance to help her out. Finally when she got home she decided to take a last look at kitty, and in it's place was a leg of lamb.

The Feline Bomb

A policeman found a box on the doorstep of the police station, abandoned & no markings on it. Being very security conscious, he called in the bomb squad to carry out a controlled explosion & destroy the package. Upon examing the remains they find the bodies of 6 kittens & a note explaining that the owner had left them there after her cat had given birth as she couldn't afford to look after them. –

Deadly Toilet Spiders

The South American Blush Spider (arachnius gluteus) has hospitalized at least three people in the Chicago area. These spiders seek out cool damp areas to nest, with the inside rim of a toilet bowl being perfect.

Actually the term "Blush Spider" refers to a small patch of varicose veins

The Deer Departed

A hunter had just bagged a deer and decided since this was the biggest he'd ever seen, let alone shot, he decided it was a Kodak moment. He used the deer's large rack to hold his rifle, set up the timer on his camera and got ready to say "cheese." The camera got several very good photos of the deer getting up and running away with the rifle.

The Deer in the Car

A hunter was returning home empty-handed from a hunting trip when he accidentally hit a deer with his car. He knew it was illegal, but decided to keep the deer anyway, and loaded it in the back of the stationwagon. As he drove down the road the "dead" deer woke up and began thrashing around in the back. The panicked driver grabbed a tire-iron and tried to hit the panicked deer in the head, but missed and hit his dog. The dog then attacked him, he swerved into the ditch and ran. He climbed up a nearby tree to escape the angry dog, and watched as the deer trashed his car.

The Dog's Dinner

An elderly couple was visiting Hong Kong and they decided to have an authentic Chinese meal. In the restaurant they couldn't make any sense of the menu, so they tried to get the waiter to decide using hand signals and expressions. They also needed some scraps for their poodle, who went with them everywhere. The waiter finally seemed to get the idea, and took the dog into the back. When he returned with the roasted dog, the couple simultaneously had heart attacks and died.

An Eyeful of Worms

There was a mentally ill woman who didn't clean her home and kept a good many pets insides, mostly cats. The animals would use the bathroom where and when ever they chose to, usually in the bedrooms of her three children. From the animal stools, the woman's oldest son got a worn egg in his eye. The worm hatched and started eating away at his eye, causing serious infections and the eye to sink back into his head. When the doctors looked at his eye, they found that the worm had laid eggs itself. The worm and eggs were removed, but his eye had to be removed and replaced with a glass eye. After that, the children were taken from the home.

The Hare Dryer

A young boy ran into his house and told his parents that the dog had killed the neighbor's pet rabbit. Hoping to avoid conflict, the father took the dirty dead rabbit from the dog, gave it a bath and a blow-dry. Then he snuck into the neighbor's yard and carefully placed the bunny back in its cage. Later that evening, after his neighbors returned home, he saw policemen and police cars next door. Worried, he casually wandered over to see what was going on. A policeman told him: "Some weirdo dug up your neighbor's dead bunny, gave it a shampoo and stuck it back in its cage. Seen any weirdoes around?"

The Honey-Child

While visiting a popular state park a man and wife spotted a bear. In order to get the perfect "photo opportunity" the parents smeared some honey on the face of their young child in the hopes of coaxing the bear into licking it off. The bear ate it along with the child's face.

Kamikaze Dogs

In World-War II Russians trained dogs by feeding them under tanks. Then they released them into battle with antitank explosives strapped to their backs. Unfortunately for the Russians, the dogs could tell the difference between Russian and German tanks, and ran under the Russian ones.

Licking the Envelope

A woman licked an envelope in a local post office and cut her tongue, after several days the place where she'd been cut began to swell. She started to get nervous and went to see a doctor. The doctor cut open the swelled area and a cockroach climbed out, there had been eggs on the envelope she had licked! -From Margaret

Love Bugs

Love-Bugs were genetically created to mate with mosquitoes and produce no offspring, but a male version was also created to keep the species alive. Since they have no natural predators their population is exploding.

The Mexican Pet

A rich old woman was visiting Mexico when a small ugly dog approached her on the sidewalk. She couldn't resist his sad eyes, so she took him back to her hotel and fed and bathed him. For the remainder of the trip the lady and her dog were inseparable. When the time came to return home, she smuggled the small dog over the border so she could keep him. Within a few days he got sick and she immediately rushed him to the vet, but there was nothing that could be done, he died in the office. After she stopped crying, the grief-stricken woman asked the vet what kind of dog he had been. The shocked vet looked at her and said: "Lady, that's no dog, it's a Mexican Sewer Rat!"

The Microwaved Pooch

An old woman had just given her little poodle a bath when she got an idea, she could dry him off in her brand-new microwave oven. It didn't seem to get very hot inside, and she'd only put him in for five minutes or so. He exploded.

Not My Dog

A young lady was invited to visit a very rich old lady's house one day for tea. She nervously rang the bell and the butler showed her in. Right away she noticed a large dirty mutt chewing the furniture enthusiastically. As she had her tea and was shown around the house by the old woman, she couldn't believe they let the dog behave the way it did. The dog chewed at the furniture, ripped the curtains and relieved himself on the carpet. The young girl didn't say anything of course, assuming that besides being rich, perhaps the old lady was also eccentric. As the woman walked her to the door she said: "I hope you'll come back again sometime, but next time PLEASE leave your dog at home."

Shooting the Bull

Some guys had heard of a good hunting spot, but needed the permission of the owner of the property. One of them went up to the farmer's house to ask if they could hunt on his land. The farmer agreed and told him that while he was out there, could he shoot the bull in the pasture for him. The hunter agreed. He decided to play a little joke on his friends and when he got in the car he told them the farmer had said no, so they were going to have to teach him a lesson. He pulled up to the field where the cows were, got his rifle and killed the bull, and said "That'll teach him." His friends jumped out of the car laughing, grabbed their guns and shot several cows before the dismayed joker could stop them. As they paid the farmer for all the cows they'd killed, he told them that if they wanted to do some more hunting, he had some pigs out back that were allot cheaper than cows.

Snakes in the Ball-Pit

A young boy was play area of a southern McDonalds, when he came out of the ball-pit he told his mother he'd been hurt there. There were several red marks on the child's legs and arms, assuming it had been some type of insects his mother took him home. By the time they got home, the red marks had swollen and before the mother could do anything the boy died. She found out later he'd been bitten repeatedly by rattlesnakes.

Sometimes it's Burger King and a different kind of snake. Maybe this one is the reason allot of fast-food places are building their play-areas inside now.

The Spider Cactus

A woman visiting Mexico bought a small cactus as a souvenir and smuggled it across the border when she went home. A few days later she was admiring her cactus when she could have sworn it wiggled a little, she dismissed it as a trick of the light until it began to vibrate. Finally she began to worry and called customs to confess her crime and see what she should do about the wiggling plant, in a panicked voice the man on the phone told her to get out of the house immediately. It was too late and by the time the men in protective clothing got there, the cactus had burst open releasing thousands of tiny spiders who made the woman their first meal

The Spider in the Hairdo

Back when all the girls wore beehive hairdos, one girl ratted her hair so high and put so much hairspray in it, that she never washed or took it down and combed it. One day in school blood began to trickle down her forehead. She was rushed to the hospital, but was dead on arrival. At some point a spider had laid eggs in her hair, they had hatched and the baby spiders had began eating her brain.

Sometimes the hairdo is an afro.

The Suicidal Dog

A young man was waiting in the high-rise apartment of his new girlfriend waiting as she finished getting ready for their date and he decided to play with her frisky little dog. He began throwing the ball for the dog and accidentally bounced it out and over the balcony, without a thought the dog followed. The man had no idea what to do or say when his date came out of the bathroom ready to go, she didn't seem to notice the dog's absence. At dinner the man commented "You know, your dog seemed a little depressed this evening."

The Trapper's Dog

A trapper lived high in the mountains with his infant son and his large sled-dog. His wife had died during childbirth, so it was up to the dog to protect the child while the trapper was out. One day the trapper was hours late returning home because of an especially heavy snow and his blood ran cold when he saw the door of his home was ajar. He grabbed his ax and rushed in to see the floor was covered in blood and the baby's crib was empty. He stared in horror as his dog crept from under the bed, his muzzle red with blood. With a cry the trapper raised his ax and buried it in the dog's head. He heard his baby crying and ran to the other side of the bed to find him alive and unharmed. He also found a dead timber-wolf clinching some of his dog's fur in his teeth.

From a Welsh legend circa the middle ages, but the trapper's a King and the dog's name is Gelert.

The Tummy Ache

Two young boys were hiking through the forest one day, and decided to drink out of a small stream they came upon. They were badly frightened by a snake nest by the water, and ran home. A year later one of the boys had to be hospitalized, he was always hungry, but stayed thin and was plagued by stomach cramps. The doctor pumped his stomach and found a full grown snake coiled inside.

Another Tummy Ache

The father of a teenage girl was growing more and more worried that his little girl's stomach seemed to be growing. Over and over she swore she couldn't be pregnant but her father was suspicious because of how much time the girl was at the beach. Finally he took her to the hospital when she started complaining about stomach pain. The doctor confirmed she wasn't pregnant, it appeared to be a tumor or growth of some kind, he said an operation was necessary immediately. Octopus eggs are microscopic, and they assumed the girl must have swallowed some while swimming.

Wall to Wall

A carpet layer had just finished with a wall to wall job when he wanted a smoke, he started looking around for his cigarettes and noticed a lump in the carpet. Frustrated and not wanting to re-do anything he grabbed a hammer and pounded the lump flat. The next day the old lady who'd hired him for the job called and told him he'd forgotten a pack of cigarettes, and asked "By the way, did you happen to see my canary while you were working, he seems to have gotten out of his cage again?"

The Cheating Bride

After a man and woman were pronounced married the groom turned to the audience and explained that under each guest's chair was an envelope with a picture of the bride having sex with the best man. He'd found out about it earlier but decided to go through with the wedding so her parents could pay for the ceremony and all their friends and family could know the truth. He got an annulment the following Monday.

The Sweet Smell of Revenge

A man had been sleeping around behind his wife's back, unknown to him she had become suspicious. When she finally found evidence she packed up and left him - taking only her most personal belongings. The man soon perked up and enjoyed his new found freedom. Soon after he noticed a bad smell through the main part of the house. Blaming the smell on bad house cleaning he set too it and scrubbed the place from top to bottom but still the smell remained. Enlisting the help of his girlfriend they checked and found, sewn into the hem of the floor length curtains, prawns - rotten and mushy. Needless to say the curtains were tossed and the ex had her moment of revenge.

What Time is it?

A guy calls his live in girlfriend and tells her he's met someone else and wants her to move out. He'll be gone all weekend and says for her to be gone by the time he gets back. He expects to find his place trashed when he arrives, but finds everything is just fine except the telephone is off the hook. He hangs it up and thinks nothing of it until he gets the phone bill. Before she left, the girlfriend called the number to "Time" in Tokyo and left the phone off the hook for two days.

"The Accidental Cannibals"

Just after World War II, in a food package sent by relatives in the United States, a family in Europe (often Eastern Europe) finds a jar of powder without a label or any note of explanation. Assuming it to be some kind of American instant drink, the family stirs spoonfuls of the powder into hot water and drinks it. In other versions the powder is used as a cooking spice or thought to be dried coconut, bread flour, or a cake mix. A letter arrives later, explaining that the jar contained the cremains of a relative who had immigrated to the States years ago, died during the war, and had wanted to be buried in his or her native country. Sometimes the explanatory letter is in the same package, but it is written in English and nobody is available to translate it until after the cremains have been eaten.

A recent version of the legend describes the cremains of a relative shipped home from Australia to England and mixed there into the Christmas pudding. Half the pudding has been consumed by the time the letter of explanation arrives.

"The Acrobatic Professor"

A professor promises his class that he will not give a surprise quiz in the course until "the day you see me come into the classroom through the transom." Then one day, after the class has arrived, their professor comes climbing through the transom with a gleeful grin on his face and a stack of quizzes clutched in one hand. It turns out that he had earlier worked as a circus acrobat. Variations on the story describe the quiz-toting professor entering through a second-story window or climbing out of a grand piano.

This story is told about a surprising number of American professors who are often named and given their correct academic specialties in these accounts, although none of these stories has yet been positively verified. Best known of the group was Guy Y. "Guy Wire" Williams (1881–1968), a chemistry professor at the University of Oklahoma (from 1906 until his death), who was described in one source as "a skilled gymnast and acrobat." However, even Williams's biographical sources do not specifically include the transom trick.

The Ultimate Urban Legends

"All That Glitters Is Not Gold"

A woman riding a Manhattan subway feels her gold neck chain being snapped loose just as the train slows down at a station. Reacting automatically, she reaches over and snaps off the chain that's around her attacker's neck, and he runs out the door and up the stairs. Later, a jeweler tells her that the chain she grabbed was pure gold. Her own chain was an inexpensive fake.

This story was heard by a New York City journalist in 1989 but could not be verified. It was included in a collection of urban legends because of its familiar unwitting-theft theme.

"The Avon Flasher"

With a "ding-dong" at the door, the Avon Lady comes to call. After delivering a mediocre sales pitch, the tall, husky traveling saleslady asks if she can use the bathroom. A short time later she calls out from the bathroom that there is no more toilet paper. Since the woman of the house had just hung a fresh roll that morning, she becomes suspicious and calls the police. The cops arrive and find a naked man lurking in her bathroom.

Like "The Hairy-Armed Hitchhiker," this legend describes a man dressed as a woman who preys on women but is foiled. Variations of this story—popular in the mid-1980s—describe a washer repairman trying to lure the woman to the basement where he awaits her naked. Sometimes there is no repairman, but the woman simply hears her washer starting up and, suspicious, calls the police.

The Avon Lady version is known in Australia and, perhaps also, as Aussie folklorist Graham Seal speculates, "wherever else in the world that Avon calls."

Babies

As innocent victims of neglect or violence, babies are killed or seriously injured in most of the urban legends in which they appear. The four entries that follow, plus other legends discussed in this book, describe babies being abandoned, abducted, killed by a rampaging animal, lost, misplaced, mutilated, neglected, roasted, slain for their organs, and otherwise poorly or cruelly treated by those responsible for their care. The guilt of the caregivers extends to parents, siblings, and baby-sitters alike, although in some instances the neglect is inadvertent and accidental rather than deliberate.

In a rare example of a legend baby *surviving* a threat, an infant in its car seat, forgotten on the car roof by a distracted parent, is spotted by an alert bystander and rescued before suffering injury. In the most horrible and cynical example of a dead-baby legend, the corpse of an infant is said to have been hollowed out in order to smuggle drugs into the United States in the arms of a supposed parent on an international flight.

"The Baby Train"

The extraordinarily high birthrate of a particular town, suburb, neighborhood, apartment building, or other dwelling area is explained by the daily passage of an early-morning train whose loud whistle awakens couples. Since it is too early to get up for work or school and too late to go back to sleep, the couples make love—and produce more "whistle babies." Some couples fail to follow the local trend because they get used to the whistle (or are hard of hearing) and stay asleep.

The baby-train legend is popular as an American college story, told about married-student apartments all across the country, but it is also known, with adaptations to local cultures, in rural America, as well as in Europe, South Africa, Australia, and probably elsewhere. The story has been traced to early Industrial Revolution lore in England when trains were just developing into major transportation devices. The same supposed universal trait of human nature is reflected in the folklore concerning allegedly high birthrates just nine months after natural disasters such as earthquakes and hurricanes have knocked out power for lengthy periods.

"The Bargain Sports Car"

The Ultimate Urban Legends

In this cheap-car fantasy, a mother finally decides to sell the old car that her son, who was killed in action, had left in her garage when he was sent to Vietnam with the military. She advertises the 1965 Chevrolet for $200 since it is ten years old and small ("It only holds two people.") Sometimes she calls a dealer to ask what a car of that age and size would be worth. A buyer who can only afford a cheap used car arrives to find that she has a classic Corvette set up on blocks and in perfect condition. He whips out his checkbook and buys it for the advertised price. Sometimes the man arrives just a few minutes too late, and he sees the Corvette being driven out of the garage by another buyer.

"The Bedbug Letter"

A businessman traveling by train on a sleeper car finds his berth infested with bedbugs. He writes to the railroad company to complain and receives a letter from the president of the company that is full of abject apologies and promises to fire the workers responsible and to clean and disinfect the sleeping cars. The letter assures him that such a thing has not happened previously and will never happen again. Still attached to this polite reply, however, is a routing slip that reads, "Send this son of a bitch the bedbug letter." Sometimes, along with the apology, the original letter is returned with the "bedbug letter" directive rubber-stamped on it.

This story is always told about the old days of railroad travel, usually the 1940s, although some people claim (without verification) that it goes back to the turn of the century when George M. Pullman still presided over the sleeping-car company that gave his name to the cars themselves. The story does not seem to have become attached to modern Amtrak sleepers.

"The Bird-Foot Exam"

The entire final examination in a college ornithology class consists of identifying a number of birds by their feet. The students are given either a page of drawings of bird feet or are shown a row of stuffed birds with bags covering all but their feet.

The students are outraged, and all except one apply themselves to the problem as best they can. The dissenter marches to the front of the room, slams his exam paper onto the professor's desk, and declares that "this is the stupidest test I've ever seen!" The professor glances at the blank examination paper and asks, "What's your name?" The student hitches up his pants leg, extends his foot, and says, "You tell me, Prof!" and stomps out of the classroom.

The themes of unreasonable testing procedures and of instructors in large colleges failing to know their individual students are both found in other academic legends.

"The Blind Man"

A woman has just undressed to take a shower when her doorbell rings. She calls out—"Who is it?"—and hears the reply, "Blind man." Assuming that a blind man would not know she is naked, she grabs a couple of dollars to make a donation (or to buy pencils or whatever he is selling) and opens the door. She thrusts the money at the man, who takes it with a surprised look and then asks, "Now where do you want me to hang these blinds?"

This story has been widely repeated for decades, both in folk tradition and by professional writers and comedians. Older versions mention Venetian blinds, as these window coverings were once called. Ann Landers published a version in 1986, commenting, "It's a funny story, whether it's true or not." She published it again in her October 13, 1998, column.

"The Boy Who Played Superman"

After viewing a Superman movie or TV program, a young boy ties a towel or curtain around his neck as a cape and jumps from a high place, believing he can fly like his hero Superman. Other such "Flights of Fancy" stories are told about children trying to fly like Mary Poppins or to demonstrate tremendous strength like Popeye.

Told by some people to demonstrate that comic books may lead to harm for suggestible children, such stories cannot usually be verified. Often the tales turn out to be merely a parent's guess about why a child dropped from a high place, or else they are misremembered news stories that do not quite match the legend.

"The Bump in the Rug"

A carpet-layer has just finished installing wall-to-wall carpeting in a home, but as he is standing back admiring the job and patting his pockets looking for his packet of cigarettes, he notices a lump in the middle of the floor. He does not find the cigarettes in his pocket, so he concludes that he must have dropped them while he was working and rolled the new carpet right over them.

He is not about to remove the new carpet just for a packet of cigarettes, so he takes a hammer from his tool box and pounds down the lump, neatly flattening it. As he puts his tools into his truck, he notices his cigarettes lying there on the dashboard. Just then the lady of the house comes out and asks, "Did you by any chance see my parakeet while you were working? It got out of its cage again."

Sometimes the missing pet is a hamster or gerbil. This story has been told among American carpet-layers and home decorators since at least the 1950s. A version appeared in *Reader's Digest* in 1964 and in *People* in 1990. "The Bump in the Rug" is also told in England, and probably in other countries as well.

Bungling Brides

A husband sees his new wife cutting a roast or a ham in half— or removing the drumsticks from a turkey—before roasting. He asks her why she does this and is told that this is how her mother always prepared such meats for roasting. Curious, the husband asks his mother-in-law about this; she explains that she simply never owned a pan large enough to accommodate a whole roast, ham, or large turkey. Variations on the theme include the bride misunderstanding the direction "leave room to rise" in a biscuit recipe or attaching small cotton balls to her screen door to repel flies (her mother had used cotton from pill bottles to plug holes in her screen door).

Although the helpless or naive bride is an outdated and sexist stereotype, such stories continue to be told, sometimes as an example of either the power of habit or of the need to question all traditions in order to learn their true sources and meanings.

Cadavers

The need to dissect human corpses in order for medical students to learn anatomy has led to hoaxes, pranks, jokes, and legends common among doctors-in-training. Many of these items involve the amputation of a limb, or even of a penis, and prankish use of this appendage. The most developed cadaver narrative tells of a medical student discovering that the body assigned to him or her for dissection is that of a recently deceased relative.

Child Ballad

This refers to any of the 305 traditional British ballads collected and published by Harvard professor Francis James Child (1825—1896) in his monumental work *The English and Scottish Popular Ballads* (1882–1898). A *ballad* is a narrative folksong—a traditional song that tells a story. Although gathered by Child primarily from manuscript and early published sources, the "Child Ballads," as they continue to be called, have also had wide circulation in oral tradition, both in Britain and the United States. Folklorists invariably refer to them by their number and title in the Child collection (e.g., Child 155, "Sir Hugh, or, the Jew's Daughter," is related to the ancient blood-libel legend and is thus part of the background of the urban legend "The Mutilated Boy"). The term "Child Ballad" has nothing whatever to do with children, either as the subjects or singers of traditional ballads.

Cigar Insurance ("Cigarson")

A man buys a full case of expensive cigars and insures them against fire. After he has smoked them all, he files a claim with the insurance company saying that they were destroyed "in a series of small fires." The company pays him—then has the man arrested for arson; he is convicted and sentenced to one year for each count. This story arose and faded on the Internet in 1996, although it is still circulated there occasionally.

The "Cigarson" story, despite being untrue, is sometimes referred to in discussions of supposed outrages in the American legal system and the need for tort reform.

"The Climax of Horrors"

A traditional European folk story (Tale Type 2040) in which a servant greets his long-absent returning master by declaring that there is "no news" to report except that the dog died. But, when questioned, the servant describes a series of catastrophes that had occurred—leading up to the death of the master's wife—and only incidentally involving the death of the dog.

The story is sometimes called "No News" or "The Dog Died" and was circulated in old schoolbooks and other printed sources as well as orally either in the form of a tale or a recitation. "The Climax of Horrors" is still occasionally told by urban storytellers somewhat in the style of a contemporary legend.

"The Colo-Rectal Mouse"

A friend of a friend knows someone working at a local hospital who supposedly was present when a homosexual man came into the emergency room to have a live mouse or other small creature removed from his rectum. He had used a greased plastic tube to insert the mouse, having heard that this would give him the ultimate sexual thrill. The string he had tied to the mouse broke when the man tried to pull it out. Sometimes a mouse skeleton is stuck inside the man, or the creature is a small lizard whose tail broke off when the man tried to pull it back out.

This story appeared in 1984 and quickly spread across the United States. The animal came to be referred to consistently as a gerbil in subsequent years when this legend was applied specifically to several male media figures who were thought by the public to be homosexual.

"The Corpse in the Car"

In a European legend of World War II, a hitchhiker predicts the death of Hitler or the end of the war on a particular date and that the person(s) who picked him up will find a corpse in the car by the end of the day. The second prediction comes true, but the first does not. Usually the corpse is that of a person whom the driver stops to help after an automobile accident; the injured person dies in the car en route to the hospital.

This "myth" was the subject of a famous psychoanalytic study by Princess Marie Bonaparte of Greece, who first heard it in September 1938 with the prediction that "Hitler will be dead in six months." The story persisted in various versions throughout the war years and was occasionally incorporated into "The Vanishing Hitchhiker." Double predictions are found in earlier traditional legends as well.

Bonaparte collected several variations of the legend, and her analysis suggested that the story demonstrated a "regression" caused by anxieties concerning the war that "must have reactivated the need to offer a human victim in propitiation to fate."

Two psychologists, Sandy Hobbs and David Cornwell, reviewed the available data and noted the "comparative neglect" of this legend by folklorists. Their study demonstrated how scholars' own comments on "The Corpse in the Car" have contributed to confusion about the definition, classification, and analysis of contemporary legends.

"The Crushed Dog"

A young man is a houseguest of a prominent family, usually people who are important to his own future. In his bedroom he accidentally spills an inkwell, spoiling a carpet or other furnishings. His attempts to clean up the mess fail, and he slips away in the night, too embarrassed to confront his hosts. Some time later he is forgiven and invited back, but this time he accidentally sits on a small dog concealed on an overstuffed chair in a dimly lit parlor. He hides the dog's body and flees again, this time never to return.

The two-episode structure of this story is unusual for urban legends. Indeed, much of the circulation of "The Crushed Dog" is in printed sources. But the story has an oral tradition as well, with variations on the reason for the overnight visit, the means by which ink was spilled, the breed of dog, where the body is hidden, and so on. Sometimes the episodes are reversed, and there are a few variations on the nondog portion of this farcical comedy.

"The Crushed Dog" illustrates the anxieties people may feel when trying to make a good impression, especially in an unsettling social situation. A few versions describe an American abroad who is intimidated and confused by foreign customs. The legend also reveals disdain for small breeds of essentially useless lapdogs that are preferred as pets by some wealthy folks.

"The Cut-Off Finger"

A woman is shopping at a large mall while her husband or boyfriend waits outside for her. But when the mall is starting to close, she still has not appeared, so he asks security to search for her. The woman is found in a fitting room where someone, often thought to be a black assailant, has cut off one of her fingers in order to steal her diamond ring. She has lost blood and has fainted, so they rush her to an emergency room for treatment. The thief is never caught.

This American legend of the mid-1970s to early 1980s, like several others, takes place in a shopping mall (or a mall parking lot). Folklorist Eleanor Wachs has interpreted the story in terms of its themes of conspicuous consumption, racial tensions, and "fear of urban crime and physical attack."

The severed-fingers theme also appears in an automobile legend of that title as well as in "The Choking Doberman." The legend of "The Hook" is about an attacker's severed hand (really its hooked substitute). Severed fingers and hands also appear in the traditional folktale "The Robber Bridegroom," also called "Mr. Fox" (Tale Type 955). An urban legend in which the attacker himself suffers injury to his finger is "The Robber Who Was Hurt."

A separate legend ("The Rider with the Extra Hand") describes the finger- or hand-lopping criminal finally being caught, usually on a bus or subway, when the severed appendage in his pocket is dripping blood and he is found to have the stolen ring or rings there as well. This story is occasionally heard in the United States but is better known abroad, including in Sweden, Spain, and Colombia.

Dental Death

When a patient dies in the chair, supposedly the dentist will carry the corpse to the restroom, leaving him to be discovered. This happens sometimes when a dentist has two treatment rooms and tries to work on patients in both chairs at once. One time a dentist had his "corpse" come walking back in, since the trip downstairs to the restroom had revived the patient, who was only deeply sedated.

Such stories stem from people's dread of dental work and distrust of dentists, but they are completely impossible, not only because of medical ethics but also because a dental assistant, receptionist, or another patient would surely observe the crime or a relative would know where the person was going that day. Besides, if such were a general practice, sooner or later a guilty dentist would be caught, leading to massive publicity.

"The Dishonest Note"

A driver returns to his parked car to find it damaged from a collision with another car leaving the lot. A note placed under the windshield wiper reads, "The people watching me think I am leaving my name and address, but I am not."

"The Dishonest Note" has been repeated as a story since the 1960s both orally and in newspaper columns, but it has also actually happened a number of times, as attested by both victims and perpetrators who have come forward. Some tellers expand on the details, describing a crowd of people watching the guilty party write the note; but nobody ever seems to have taken down his license-plate number.

"The Dog in the High-rise"

A man comes to pick up his date, who lives in an apartment in a high-rise. While she is getting ready in another room, he tosses a ball for her dog to fetch. On the third throw the ball bounces out the open door, onto the balcony, and over the railing into the street far below. The dog jumps after the ball.

Writer Truman Capote told this story frequently as a true story about a model, her blind date, and her Great Dane, but other versions, usually about smaller breeds of dogs, also circulate. Similar to "The Crushed Dog," this legend describes a pet's unfortunate death as a result of a nervous visitor's faux pas. The plot has been used in at least two TV productions, one a sitcom episode and the other a beer commercial.

"The Dolly Parton Diet"

In 1981 the story spread orally and by means of photocopies that Dolly Parton had lost weight following a strict diet that consisted of essentially all you wanted to eat of one food each day, plus servings of "T. J.'s Miracle Soup." Numerous people, mainly in the Midwest, followed the diet, some claimed with great success. None reported any enlargement of bust size, a stated hope of some women who had tried the diet.

Some copies of this diet were titled "The Hollywood Diet" or claimed that it had been developed by "Sacred Heart Hospital–Spokane." A parody called "The Stress Diet" was circulating at about the same time; this one began each day with a light breakfast, then progressed through the day with more and more cookies, pizza, beer, and snacks. The parody also included a list of "Diet Tips" such as, "If no one sees you eat it, it has no calories" and "Snacks consumed in a movie don't count."

Ricki Fulman's investigative article on this story in the *New York News* is a case study in debunking an oral tradition by means of following up on each person's stated source. Fulman's search found no verification for the story, only a chain of friends of friends, and she concluded that "after interrogating close to 50 persons about this, enough is enough."

Drug Horror Stories

Rumors and stories grossly exaggerate the dangerous effects of drugs, particularly LSD and PCP (known on the street as "angel dust"). The most common "mythic tale," as one investigator has labeled them, is that a group of college students in the 1960s, high on LSD, stared directly into the sun until they lost their eyesight. A similar story claims that people high on PCP have plucked out their own eyes. Other violent self-destructive behavior supposedly typical of crazed drug users includes jumping off roofs and extracting their own teeth; some addicts allegedly gained enough strength when high on drugs to tear themselves free from locked handcuffs. Stories of users cooking babies or of smugglers using an infant's hollowed-out corpse to smuggle drugs are also part of the drug horror story tradition.

As bad as drug addiction and drug crimes are in today's world, none of the above stories is literally true. Still, they are sometimes repeated by antidrug groups and even by police authorities as dire warnings against the evils of drug use.

"The Exploding Bra"

A woman (sometimes a flight attendant) is wearing an inflatable brassiere on an airplane trip. As the cabin pressure changes, her bra expands alarmingly. She rushes for the restroom, sometimes making it in time to deflate her bra discreetly, but in other versions the bra explodes en route. Alternately, the inflated bra may be stuck with a pin—either by the wearer trying to stop the extra expansion, or (in nonairplane versions) by a young man pinning a corsage onto his date's dress.

Inflatable bras do, of course, exist, but the stories of surprising expansion due to changing air pressure are highly doubtful and always told second- or thirdhand. Similar stories are sometimes told about silicon breast implants, although the claims for their further expansion are even more dubious with these products.

"The Failed Suicide"

A desperate man tries to arrange multiple, simultaneous methods to bring about his own death, but they cancel out one another. For example, the man may stand on a high cliff above the sea with a noose around his neck tied to a tree, a loaded gun in one hand, and a vial of poison in the other. He drinks the poison, fires the gun toward his head, and jumps; but the shot severs the rope, he survives the fall, and the seawater that he swallows causes him to vomit up the poison. He swims to shore.

A less complicated version of the story describes a man leaping from a high window after having an argument with his wife in their apartment or being fired by his boss. The would-be suicide lands on top of his wife (or his boss, who has gone out for lunch after the unpleasant job of firing the man). The wife (or boss) dies, but the man lives.

Variations of these stories have circulated orally, in typescript, and on the Internet but are also published from time to time, sometimes to illustrate human behavior, the random nature of events, legal and moral aspects of suicide, and the like. One such printing by a British expert on forensic medicine described the multiple-means-of-death version as "a classic of its kind... not susceptible to confirmation."

"The Fallen Angel Cake"

This story was published in 1980 in a Sydney, Australia, newspaper and, in 1982, in a slightly different version in a small-town Canadian newspaper. Both reports described it as an actual incident well known to the local population, so probably it is a widespread apocryphal account, that is, a modern legend. Less likely—indeed barely possible—is that the same mishap occurred twice in far distant places.

A woman bakes an angel food cake for her church's bake sale, but when it comes out of the oven the center of the cake collapses. Lacking time to make a second cake, the woman uses a roll of toilet paper to build up the center of her cake, and she frosts over the whole thing. She rushes her cake to the church sale, then gives her daughter some money and instructs her to hurry to the sale, buy it back, and bring it directly home. But the daughter arrives too late; the cake has already been sold. The next day the cake-baker goes to her bridge club, and she finds that the hostess has bought her cake and is serving it for dessert. Before the woman can warn her, the hostess acknowledges a compliment on the beautiful cake, saying, "Thank you. I baked it myself."

"The Flying Kitten"

A couple's new kitten climbs to the top of a small birch tree in their yard and stays there. In order to rescue it, the owners throw a rope across a high branch and pull the top of the tree down; but the rope slips or breaks, and the kitten is launched high into the air and over their fence. The couple are unable to find the kitten. A week or so later, one of the kitten's former owners is in a supermarket and meets a neighbor who is buying cat food. "I didn't know you had a cat," says the first shopper. "We didn't, until last week when the cutest little kitten just fell out of the air and into my husband's lap."

This story was reported in a 1987 *Washington Post* article as told by a woman who heard it as a "true story" by her hairdresser. Several other versions have been collected, both from published and oral sources. Cats, of course, are the subjects of numerous urban legends, and in many of these stories the felines suffer some kind of harm or trauma, though often landing on their feet and surviving.

"The Girl on the Gearshift Lever"

A boy slips some Spanish Fly (*Lytta vesicatoria,* or dried blister beetles, also known as cantharis, believed to be an aphrodisiac), into his date's drink while they are at a drive-in movie. But he has unwittingly overdosed her with twice the amount required for good results. When he returns to the car from buying popcorn, he discovers that in her sexual eagerness the girl has impaled herself on the gearshift lever, sometimes with fatal results.

This story, also called "Stick-Shift Frenzy," was well known in the 1950s when four-on-the-floor shifters and drive-in movies were more common. Other seduction stories have replaced it in recent years.

"The Golf Bag"

A golfer, angry at his poor play after hitting several consecutive shots into a pond on the eighteenth hole, in full view of the clubhouse crowd, flings his golf bag into the pond and stalks off the course. A few minutes later, the same group notices him walking back to the pond. They watch as he uses a groundskeeper's rake to fish out the bag, extract his car keys from a zippered pocket, throw it back into the water, then head again for the parking lot.

This story is repeated as a true incident, both about local golfers and about certain short-fused celebrities, but never about golf professionals.

"The Good Times Virus"

Perhaps the most widespread bogus computer-virus warning, and certainly the most thoroughly debunked and parodied, was the "Good Times" virus alert of the mid-1990s. Countless warnings were circulated via e-mail and in publications warning that a message with the subject line "Good Times" or its attached file contained a virus that could do irreparable harm to one's personal computer and its files. Computer experts unanimously branded the warnings a hoax, implying deliberate misinformation spread by a malicious individual or group. Another viewpoint might be that it was simply a joke, mistaken for a real warning by a public accustomed to receiving similar bogus warnings and never knowing whether to believe them or not. (The fact that real computer viruses can spread via e-mail attachments was proven in March 1999 with the appearance of the notorious and damaging "Melissa" virus.)

The most pointed parody of the "Good Times" warning—among many—described the "Bad Times" virus that would (among numerous other attacks) "scratch any CDs you try to play" and "give your ex-wife your new phone number."

The Gremlin Effect

The French phrase *l'effet gremlins* (the gremlin effect), coined in 1992 by Jean-Bruno Renard, refers to modern rumors and legends describing supposed dangers of new technologies, including such themes as "welded" contact lenses, people being "cooked" by tanning-salon lamps, power lawnmower accidents, and deaths or harm caused by microwave ovens. Renard borrowed the term from the 1984 American film *Gremlins,* which in turn had taken it from U.S. Air Force slang referring to imagined mischievous sprites that are said to be the causes of unexplained mechanical failures.

As Renard explained in his 1999 book *Rumeurs et légendes urbaines* (p. 101), the gremlin effect, typically, may take three different forms. Narratives may describe either misuse of an appliance (as when a microwaved poodle explodes); a defective appliance (as when stray microwaves from a home oven are said to cause sterility), or hidden injurious effects (as when microwave ovens are said to alter the structure of foods, rendering them poisonous).

Renard suggested that the gremlin effect appears not during the initial period of a technological innovation (when the product is little known and users are few), but rather during a period of "exponential growth" as the product becomes cheaper and users reach 50 percent of all potential consumers. Once the new product is well integrated into everyday life and most people feel comfortable using it, the stories that display this effect fade away.

"The Grocery Scam"

An elderly woman pushing a shopping cart full of groceries keeps staring at a young man shopping at the same supermarket. In the checkout line she tearfully explains that he looks just like her son who had been killed fighting in Vietnam, and she asks the young man if he will just call out "Goodbye, Mom!" to her when she waves at him as she leaves the store. He agrees to this. When he reaches the cashier with his few purchases, the total of his bill is enormous, and he is told that his "Mom" said that he would be paying for her groceries as well. His protests fall on deaf ears, since the checkout clerk had heard him say "Goodbye, Mom!"

Sometimes the scam takes place in a restaurant, and the victim may be a young woman (who supposedly resembles the older woman's late daughter). This story, known in Canada and Australia as well as the United States, may describe an actual scam with the two parties in cahoots in order to cheat the store or restaurant. There are also reports of impecunious actors or comedians using a similar trick to get free meals in restaurants. One person at a table leaves early, waves back at his friends, and tells the cashier, "The guy who's waving back at me is paying for my meal."

"The Guilty Dieter"

A woman who is on a strict diet has bought only a cup of black coffee at a cafeteria. A nearby diner who has eaten one of the two sugared doughnuts on his plate leaves the other behind as he stands and then walks away from the table. The dieter—ravenous—gobbles down the abandoned doughnut but looks up just in time to see the other diner returning with a second cup of coffee. The embarrassed guilty dieter has powdered sugar spilled on her chin and chest.

This story, sometimes told at Weight Watchers and other diet-group meetings, is similar to "The Package of Cookies," another legend about unintended food theft in an eatery of some kind.

Hair Turned White

This is a traditional international folk narrative motif (F1041.7, *Hair turns gray from terror*) that surfaces in some modern horror legends. The dark hair of a terrified person is said to have turned snow-white immediately (or overnight) from the shock. The modern motif occurs especially in legends about elevator accidents, specifically in "The Boyfriend's Death" and "The Giant Catfish."

"The Hairdresser's Error"

A female hairdresser is prevailed upon to cut the hair of a man who shows up at her shop just at closing time. He explains that he is on a business trip, staying at a nearby hotel, and needs to look good for an important meeting the next morning. She fastens a sheet around his neck and reaches for her tools, then notices an up-and-down motion under the middle of the sheet—right in the man's lap. Jumping to the conclusion that he is masturbating, the hairdresser hits the man hard enough with a hair dryer to knock him out; then she dials 911 and asks for help.

Handwriting on the Wall

This is a classic folk narrative motif (F1036, *Hand from heaven writes on wall*). It also appears in the Bible (Daniel 5:5). It may underlie the modern legend motif of a significant message found written on a wall or a mirror. In "AIDS Mary" the message informs a victim that he has contracted the dread sexually transmitted disease, and in "The Licked Hand" plus some versions of "The Roommate's Death" the mirror-message mocks survivors after the murder of their companions the night before. In these contemporary legends the message is usually written in lipstick or blood.

"The Hapless Water-skier"

A water-skier in a southern reservoir gets too close to an area of sunken stumps and fences. He falls, and when the boat returns to pick him up the skier says he must have hit some barbed wire, as he can feel sharp punctures in his legs. When he is pulled from the water it turns out that he had fallen into a huge ball of water moccasins; shortly afterward he dies from the multiple snakebites.

Some form of this story is told about numerous lakes, especially in the South and Midwest. Water moccasins, also called cottonmouths, are quiet creatures, seldom seen, and not believed—at least by herpetologists—to live or travel in large groups. In fact, these snakes are not even known to exist in many of the lakes where hapless water-skiers are said to have perished.

"The Helpful Mafia Neighbor"

Also known as "A Friend of the Family," this legend describes a couple who move to an expensive suburb and who find their home burglarized when they return from a weekend trip. When they ask their new neighbors if they had noticed any suspicious activity, the neighbors—soft spoken and well dressed—advise them not to report the crime to the police until they "make a few phone calls and see what can be done." Apparently the neighbors have good connections, because the next morning the burglary victims find all their possessions piled neatly on their front porch.

Although the suburban version is told in several large American cities as a recent occurrence, similar stories of stolen goods being returned after a discreet inquiry by a friend or acquaintance have circulated since the 1930s, sometimes said to have taken place in a foreign country. Older American versions imply that the helpful person had Stateside gangland connections, not necessarily Mafia-related.

"The Holy Place"

Although members of a Catholic congregation always kneel and cross themselves at a certain point in one of the church aisles, nobody knows why. An older member of the congregation provides the explanation: Years before there had been an obstruction at that spot, and anyone walking by had to duck. Eventually this evolved into genuflecting, even after the obstruction was removed.

A similar military story also illustrates the power of tradition in maintaining a meaningless ritual. A soldier is always assigned to an artillery piece during firing to stand with one hand held straight out from his shoulder. Why? The job was left over from the days of horse-drawn cannons; the soldier's assignment then was to hold the horses so they would not bolt and run when the weapon was fired.

"The Hunter's Nightmare"

An unsuccessful hunter happens to hit a deer with his car while driving home. Although it is illegal to do so, he stops and puts the deer into the backseat of his car, affixing his state hunting tag to it. But the deer was only stunned; it revives and begins kicking and struggling to escape. The man swings at the deer with a tire iron but hits his hunting dog instead, and then the dog begins to attack him. The man stops the car, jumps out pursued by his dog, escapes into a telephone booth, and calls 911, telling the police that he is trapped in the booth and that a deer is destroying the inside of his car.

Numerous individuals and police departments have copies of what is said to be the original 911 audiotape recording the hunter's panicky call for help, which is often claimed to have happened between 1989 and 1992 in the local area. However, the only documented case of this kind occurred in Poughkeepsie, New York, in 1974, and not all of the tapes circulating have the same wording or details, although most are peppered with the same range of obscenities. Exaggerated claims are made for the number of copies of the tape in existence and for the interest in it on the part of U.S. government agencies. An older tradition of stunned-animal stories exists as well. It seems likely that dubbed and faked copies of the 1974 "stunned-deer/deer-stunt" tape have been passed around and that those who have heard it have assumed that the incident happened locally and recently. Attention to the story by newspaper columnists has encouraged this notion.

"The Kangaroo Thief"

The Australian version of "The Deer Departed" claims that a group of tourists in a rented car hits a kangaroo on the road.

They stop and prop up the animal against a fencepost, dressing it in the jacket of one of the men in order to take a gag photo. But the kangaroo was merely stunned, and when the tourists step back to focus the camera the animal revives and bounds away into the outback, still wearing the jacket, which contains the passport, travelers' checks, tickets, money, and other belongings of the owner.

This story has been attributed to a touring English cricket team, to the folksong group the Kingston Trio, and to various foreign yacht-racing crews competing in Australia. Australian folklorists have traced ancestors of "The Kangaroo Thief" as far back as 1902, identifying it as an old "bush yarn" that developed into a contemporary legend. A 1992 collection of Dutch urban legends describes how a group of tourists from the Netherlands suffered the "kangaroo's revenge."

"The Leashed Dogs"

When a family on vacation stops for a break, someone puts out a water dish for the family dog and ties the pet's leash to the back bumper of the car or camper. Unfortunately, the dog is forgotten when the family drives off again, and it is dragged behind the vehicle to its death.

Or a family member at home ties the dog's leash to the garage-door handle. Another member, driving home, while still a couple of blocks away, activates the remote control to open the garage door. The pet is lynched.

Although there are claimed witnesses to both pet tragedies— or at least to incidents that are very similar—most of the retellings are attributed to friends of friends and vary in their details. In the first-person tellings, the pet usually survives, while in the second-hand stories the pet almost invariably dies, sometimes (in the vehicle version of the story) not even being missed by the family until they arrive home from vacation. Speaking of which, the 1983 film *National Lampoon's Vacation* depicted a camper version of the legend.

"The Lost Wreck"

The Ultimate Urban Legends

An automobile-accident story debunked in an Edmonton, Alberta, newspaper in 1985 seems to incorporate a key motif borrowed from a Norwegian legend collected in 1835. In the Norse story a medieval village decimated by the bubonic plague is rediscovered in a remote overgrown forest when a hunter's arrow goes astray and clangs against the church bell. In the Canadian legend a car accident of the 1950s on a mountain road in which four people were killed is discovered decades later when highway workers push some large rocks into a ravine and hear the clang of the rocks striking metal. The newspaper reporter commented "this rumor seems to have sprung from a fertile imagination fed by the clean mountain air."

The similarity of the two audible "discovery" motifs strongly suggests that this element of the modern story was borrowed from Norwegian folklore, possibly coming from the memory of a Norwegian settler in Alberta. Accounts of real-life lost-wreck incidents, of course, do not contain this traditional folkloric motif.

Masturbating into Food

A disgruntled employee of a restaurant or café—usually a fast-food franchise—masturbates into the food before serving it or sending it out for delivery. Often the perpetrator is said to be a victim of AIDS who wants revenge against society for ignoring his plight or seeks revenge against his employers for mistreating or firing him.

This story has plagued businesses selling everything from donuts to coleslaw since at least the early 1980s, but in recent years it has focused especially on Burger King ("Hold the mayo!") and Domino's Pizza ("Hold the mozzarella!"). Other franchises also mentioned in the stories include Hardees, Taco Bell, and Pizza Hut.

Earlier versions of the story were little more than rumors along the lines of, "I heard that some guy was [doing something]… at [name of place]." Later the story acquired more narrative elements, such as a description of the man's motives and methods and an account of his telephoning the

145

victims after their food has been delivered and admitting—anonymously—to his deed. The revenge of an AIDS sufferer is a motif also found in "AIDS Mary," and contamination of food is a widespread legendary theme with many variations.

"The Nude Bachelor"

When the delivered morning newspaper bumps against the front door of his home or apartment, the bachelor has just stepped out of the shower. Wearing only a towel or less, he cautiously reaches outside to get the paper, but the doorknob slips from his hand, and he is stranded outside. The man is naked, without a key, and usually has only the newspaper to cover himself with. In other versions the naked man may have been staying with his girlfriend or stepping out of his apartment to drop a letter down the mail slot or to dispose of garbage in a chute. In the versions when the man is locked out of his house, he may try to gain entry through a window, sometimes by climbing a nearby tree; neighbors, seeing a naked man lurking around, call the police.

"The Nude Bachelor" is documented in Europe, particularly Eastern Europe, since 1960 and was incorporated into literature and films there. The story became localized and well known in the United States by the next decade, and it was mirrored in a "Garfield" cartoon in 1987.

Several people report similar personal experiences. For example, in his 1969 book *Ambassador's Journal,* John Kenneth Gailbraith described a very similar personal experience, which he said happened to him in 1960 in a hotel. Luckily, a friend of his was outside the room waiting for the elevator, and he loaned Galbraith his coat to wear while waiting for a hotel employee to arrive with a passkey.

"The Obligatory Wait"

Numerous college and university students, and even a few professors and administrators, believe that a campus regulation specifies how long a class must wait for a late instructor to arrive in the classroom. Sometimes there is a sliding scale indicating the number of minutes to wait, depending upon the rank of the course's instructor—from five minutes for a graduate assistant up to 20 minutes for a full professor. Some campusfolk insist that the obligatory wait rule may be found spelled out in official college regulations, but so far nobody has located a copy of that particular rule.

It is true that some instructors do announce their personal policies regarding lateness of either students or themselves, but this is strictly an informal and unofficial action. New students generally learn about "The Obligatory Wait" via the grapevine from older students, some of whom will "prove" that the rule exists by citing either a friend of a friend or else instances when one of their classes decided to wait so-many minutes for a late professor.

Organ Thefts

Although there is some truth in the stories about thefts or sales of human organs in Third World countries for use in transplants, the persistent rumors and legends about organ-theft crime rings at work in other countries are simply urban legends. Medical ethics, the registration and assignments of organs for transplanting, the need for proper tissue, and blood-type matches and several other factors all argue against the theft of organs from random victims. The legend-form of this notion is usually called "The Kidney Heist."

"The Pet Nabber"

A small pet—often a Chihuahua, a miniature dachshund, or a toy poodle and usually belonging to tourists—is snatched by a large bird, generally an eagle, an owl, or a pelican. Such things *do* happen, although the more likely predators on pets in many regions might be coyotes. In Australia the pet-nabber story has become so prevalent that folklorist Bill Scott titled his 1996 compilation *Pelicans and Chihuahuas and Other Urban Legends.*

In 1993 the Associated Press distributed a doubtful story datelined Valdez, Alaska, about an eagle carrying off a "Chihuahua-like" dog belonging to a tourist couple traveling in a camper during a gas stop. Supposedly, while the wife was lamenting the loss of her pet, the husband stood on the other side of the camper chopping his hands in the air and muttering "Yeah! Yeah!" Yet another version of the story describes the demise of a small dog held by a tourist at a Marineland show; when a piece of meat is tossed into the tank during the shark feeding time, the dog leaps from its master's arms into the tank and is gobbled up before their eyes.

Poetic Justice

Several urban legends illustrate the idea that people receive just what they deserve, whether punishment for bad behavior or (less commonly) rewards for doing good. A typical scenario in such stories is that a thief steals something of presumed value and ends up with something that is completely worthless and even shocking. Three examples involving theft: a nicely wrapped package that is snatched contains a cat's corpse; the tempting load on a stolen car's roof turns out to be a dead grandmother; the liquid contents of a stolen whiskey bottle is only a urine sample.

In "The Loaded Dog" and "The Plant's Revenge," a person who tortures an animal or destroys a plant is injured, or even killed, by the object of his attack. "The $50 Porsche" and several other stories depict an act of revenge against an offending spouse or a companion, and "The Videotaped Theft" and "Urban Pancake" depict thieves being detected and then receiving their just deserts. Pride preceding a fall, a variation of the poetic-justice theme, is illustrated in legends like "The Unstealable Car" and "The Blind Date," although the latter might also be considered to show how bad behavior may be punished.

Among the legends that illustrate good works being rewarded are "The Will" and "The Unexpected Inheritance," in both of which a person gains a valuable inheritance from some random act of kindness or affection.

Of course, there are many other legends in which no rewards or punishments are meted out, but someone merely becomes the victim of crime, an accident, or some other threat. The people hurt in "The Kidney Heist," "AIDS Mary," "Lights

Out!" or "The Double Theft," for example, can hardly be said to deserve their fates for merely showing poor judgment or being careless.

"The Pregnant Shoplifter"

A news story circulated nationwide in February 1985 claimed that a pregnant woman in Arlington, Virginia, had been detained and searched by a sporting-goods store's personnel under suspicion of attempting to steal a basketball by concealing it under her clothes. To some journalists and folklorists this seemed too neat, too much like a legend, and, in short, "too good to be true." The story appeared to be an obvious variation of the legend about "The Shoplifter and the Frozen Food" in which a would-be thief conceals frozen food under his or her hat but is caught when either the product begins to melt or the thief faints from the cold while standing in the checkout line to buy an inexpensive item.

However, "The Pregnant Shoplifter" proved to be an authentic news story, eventually well covered in the press with names, dates, and other validating details furnished. The woman filed suit against the store for false arrest and negligence, seeking both compensatory and punitive damages. As reported in the *Washington Post* (November 19, 1986), she lost in court, but that does not mean her case is a genuine urban legend. (Still, a word-of-mouth story telling of a woman trying to steal a watermelon from a supermarket by hiding it under her dress and claiming to be pregnant has *not* been verified. Life and legend come very close together in such incidents and stories.)

'R' Is for Race"

A technologically challenged driver is confused about the meanings of the letters marked on the gear shift of his new car. He interprets "D" for "Drag," "L" for "Leap," and "N" for "Nothing." Then, while racing on the highway with another hot new car, he shifts into "R" for "Race," and his transmission blows up. In a variant version, the driver selects "P" for "Pass." ("R" actually denotes "Reverse," and "P" denotes "Park.")

149

This incident is often attributed to a young driver, a woman, or to a minority person who is supposedly unfamiliar with automotive advances. In one version the driver is the chauffeur for a southern state official. The story was popular as a legend when automatic transmission was a relatively new option, and a few early models actually had reverse placed between drive and low. In later years, the story was told more as a joke than a legend. The southern comedian Brother Dave Gardner, popular in the 1950s and 1960s, told it as a regular part of his standup routine. Yet another variation of the story describes a man teaching his wife to drive; she asks if "D" is for "Dirt Roads" and "P" is for "Pavement."

"The Rattle in the Cadillac"

As a prank, or because of some disgruntlement with management, an assembly-line worker at a luxury-automobile factory sabotages a new car by putting something inside a door panel that will rattle annoyingly when the car is driven. He adds a note taunting the owner, should he ever locate the source of the rattle. The car is not always a Cadillac, and the wording of the note varies (e.g., "So you finally found it, you SOB!" or "Aha! You found me!"). The stowaway objects may be a pop bottle, nuts and bolts, or miscellaneous trash, sometimes being suspended inside the panel on a string. There are some claims that the prank has actually been carried out, but it is certainly so much idle talk around automobile factories rather than a frequent real occurrence. Some versions of the story conclude with the wealthy car owner framing the junk and the note, displaying them in his plush office, presumably as a sort of trophy commemorating his victory over the blue-collar worker-saboteur.

"The Sawed-Off Fingers"

A factory worker operating a power saw or another piece of heavy equipment accidentally saws or slices off a finger. When someone asks him how it happened, he gestures toward the machine and says, "Like this!" and he loses a second finger or a thumb. The number of fingers lost varies, and sometimes it is toes removed by a posthole digger.

Also referred to as "Give Me a High Three," this story has been around since at least the turn of the century. Sometimes the worker is distracted by a pretty woman who is on a factory tour; she asks him how he lost his finger, and he demonstrates. Told as a joke rather than a legend, the same story may be narrated in an immigrant dialect, often Swedish ("Voops! Dere goes anudder vun!") and set in a Midwestern sawmill.

"The Secret Ingredient"

In the 1970s and 1980s the story spread, especially among fundamentalist Christian groups in the United States, that collagens taken from fetuses of aborted babies were being used in the manufacture of cosmetics. It was claimed that these "youth-preserving" products depended upon the slaughter of millions of unborn babies annually in foreign countries and that the resulting beauty products were sold widely in the United States

The flood of pamphlets, letters to newspapers, and broadcast talk shows making the secret-ingredient claim became so great that in 1985 the Food and Drug Administration issued a statement denying the rumors and stories and explaining that while protein substances are sometimes collected from placentas ("the after-birth of normal childbirth)" or from animals, no use of human fetuses as a source was documented, either in the United States or abroad.

Prodded by readers, the advice columnist Ann Landers wrote three columns debunking the secret-ingredient story in 1985. Her conclusion—that the story lacked "a shred of truth" and was "unadulterated garbage"—probably succeeded in killing the claims for good.

"Sex in the Classroom"

Various rumors and stories circulate about sex-education classes and sexy comments or situations occurring in high school or college classes. There are claims that some teachers have demonstrated sexual behavior to students, or have had students "practice" having sex. Another charge is that sex education has led to sexual experimentation or even sex crimes. A more developed story concerns an instructor who asks a double-entendre question deliberately to embarrass female students: "What part of the body is wet with hair around it and expands when needed?" The "correct" answer is the eye. Yet another variation on the theme has an instructor playfully calling his pop quizzes "quizzees"; a female student comments, unthinkingly, "Well, I'd hate to see your 'testees.'"

The sex-in-the-classroom story with the longest documented history can be traced to an anecdote about a Cambridge University anthropologist who died in 1940. Supposedly he was lecturing about a native group's customs and mentioned that women propose marriage in their traditions. When a group of female students from an affiliated college rose to leave in order to catch their bus, he quipped, "No hurry, there won't be a boat for some weeks." This was eventually converted into a very well known story told on countless other professors both in England and abroad about a lecturer mentioning the extraordinary size of the penises of men in a certain African tribe. ("The boat won't leave for Africa until next week.")

"The Shocking Videotape"

A home video of a couple who taped themselves having sex is accidentally made public, usually because they returned the wrong tape in a rental box. The couple are either husband and wife and prominent socialites, or an unmarried couple cheating on their spouses. Often the pairing is a teacher with his or her student or a coach with a team member. Sometimes the tape is being shared around a TV station when it is accidentally broadcast.

Unverified rumors and stories about amateur X-rated videotapes going public have been around nearly as long as home camcorders have been available. Few people who repeated the claims had actually seen the tapes. But there are also some well-documented cases of actual incidents of this kind, and such tapes definitely do exist. One such incident involving a law enforcement officer was reported from Kansas by *Time* magazine in its October 29, 1990, edition; another involving a University of Minnesota coach was covered in detail by the Minneapolis *Star Tribune* with the resolution of the case described in the edition of May 20, 1998.

"The Shoplifter and the Frozen Food"

In the versions of this story told in Europe since the 1970s, a person is caught trying to smuggle a frozen chicken out of a supermarket by hiding it under his or her hat. The shoplifter is caught either when the bird begins to thaw, sending rivulets of blood down the neck, or else when he or she faints from the chilled brain. In American versions of the story the item stolen may be some other kind of frozen food or a steak, and the thief is often described as a poor person, often elderly.

Another legend in which food on the head leaks out is "The Brain Drain." Prototypes for that legend, plus other stories about stolen goods hidden in one's hat, suggest that both stories may be derived from much older narratives.

"Shrink-to-Fit Jeans"

Supposedly a teenager was squeezed to death when he or she sat in a bathtub filled with water wearing a new pair of jeans, hoping to shrink them to a snug fit. The family won a huge cash settlement from the company.

"The Smashed VW Bug"

Two giant semi trucks collide and, from the force of the accident, are literally fused together. The trucks are hauled away in one big piece to a wrecking yard. Days or weeks later when the debris is separated to reclaim the scrap metal, a Volkswagen Beetle (nicknamed the "Bug") is discovered smashed between the two trucks with the flattened remains of a driver and sometimes more individuals inside. Versions of the story vary as to the location of the accident, the direction the trucks were traveling, the number of victims, and how the deaths were discovered (sometimes from a terrible odor emanating from the wreck).

In another variation of the story a VW is struck by a large truck without the truck driver noticing. The VW is found hours later still stuck like a real bug to the front of the other vehicle. Both versions of the smashed-Bug story are found in Europe and the United States. These gruesome yarns, which reflect a modicum of truth about actual accidents, serve to underscore the relative safety of large heavy vehicles versus compact cars in highway accidents. The focus on the popular Volkswagen Beetle rather than some other small car suggests the influence of the "Goliath effect," although perhaps considering the size of the car it might better be called the "David effect" in this instance.

"The Snake in the Strawberry Patch"

In the summer of 1987 a localized version of the old "bosom serpent" legend spread through North Carolina and Virginia, as reported in several regional newspapers. Supposedly, a baby had been fed some milk, then left sleeping by the side of the field while its mother picked strawberries. A snake, attracted by the smell of milk on the baby's breath, crept up to the child and slithered down its throat, strangling the baby. Both the supposed attraction of snakes to milk and the snake's approach occurring when the victim is asleep in the outdoors are motifs found in the older legend, which must have migrated to the United States from Europe where it has been well known for centuries.

"Snakes in the Tunnel of Love"

Snakes and other creatures hidden in amusement rides is a major theme in legends (see the entry "Amusement Park Dangers"). Watersnakes—especially water moccasins (or "cottonmouths")—are said to infest the streams through which little boats move, as in the tunnel of love, the log flume, and similar rides. Often it is said that a rider has dangled his or her hand over the side into the water, where it is bitten by a snake with fatal results. The couple emerge from the tunnel at the end of the ride with one party dead.

"The Suppressed Product"

The best-known manifestation of this theme in urban legends is "The Economical Car" in which an advanced experimental

automobile that gets phenomenal mileage is accidentally sold,
then recovered by the manufacturer and kept out of production
so as to preserve profits for big oil companies. A variation on
this theme claims that a pill has been developed that will
extend gas mileage or even render a tank full of water usable
as fuel in a gasoline engine. Other suppressed products
mentioned in rumors and legends include razor blades, light
bulbs, and batteries that never wear out.

"Take My Tickets, Please!"

In an American city with a losing professional team (usually
football or baseball), a man has two tickets to the next game
but no real desire to watch another debacle. He places his
tickets in plain sight on the dashboard of his car and leaves the
window open as he shops at a mall, expecting that someone
will steal the tickets. However, when he returns to his car he
finds that someone has left two more game tickets next to his
own. The number of tickets may vary, and sometimes the
story is told about a college team.

Technical Incompetence

A favorite theme in contemporary legends is that of a
technically challenged person failing to understand how some
modern device works, which leads to dangerous results that
are often humorous as well. Often the naive user is said to be
an especially young or old person, a woman, a minority
member, or an immigrant. The implication is that "normal"
white male Americans are perfectly capable to using
technology properly, whereas "others" are stereotyped as
being baffled by technology.

The devices that baffle the challenged individuals range from
computers, microwave ovens ("The Microwaved Pet"), and
tanning beds ("Curses! Broiled Again!") to automatic
transmission ("Push-Starting the Car") and cruise control. The
victims in these legends may suffer a computer crash, the loss
of a pet, a deadly cancer, or an automobile accident. Other
devices about which a few doubtful rumors and stories
circulate are ATMs, remote controls, keyless entries, smoke
alarms, and fax machines.

"The Unexpected Inheritance"

Referred to generically as "Promiscuity Rewarded" and in a distinctive Irish version as "The Kilkenny Widow," this legend describes two men staying overnight at a small hotel or rooming house owned by a beautiful young widow. One man slips off to the bedroom of the widow, at her invitation, where he spends the night. Some months later, the other man receives word that the widow has died and left him a considerable fortune. It turns out that the first man had used the second man's name during his romantic rendezvous.

Variations of this story were told in Ireland in the early 1980s, published in *Reader's Digest* in August 1989, and appeared in a *New York Times* article in 1985. In the first of these versions the incident is credited to a small hotel in the village of Kilkenny. The second version describes two American tax agents having a car breakdown in an unspecified rural area, and the third sets the incident in a sleeping car on an Italian train in which a married *woman* gives another person's name to the man with whom she spends the night.

"The Unlucky Contact Lenses"

Two people are sleeping in the same bed, or at least in the same room. One of them puts his or her contact lenses into a half-full glass of water for the night and leaves the glass on a bedside table. The other sleeper awakens in the middle of the night with a strong thirst; he or she fumbles for the water glass and drinks it dry—contact lenses and all.

This story is told on a variety of persons, including husbands and wives, lovers, prostitutes and their customers, and members of athletic teams on the road. A number of firsthand accounts of actual swallowed contacts have been reported, but the extended versions of the story involving celebrities, love affairs, prostitutes, and the like seem, as they say, "too good to be true." Some versions of the story describe a person swallowing his or her own contacts, but this seems even a more unlikely scenario than the others. Besides, how many contact wearers leave their lenses in a plain glass of water by the bedside overnight?

"The Unzipped Plumber or Mechanic"

In both typical versions of this legend a wife, returning from shopping, sees a man whom she presumes to be her husband working under the sink ("Unzipped Plumber") or under his car ("Unzipped Mechanic"). Only his legs are sticking out, and she playfully unzips his fly and fondles him. Soon afterward the wife discovers her husband in the house reading the paper, and she learns that he had given up on the repair job he was doing and summoned a professional. They rush to the aid of the other man and find him knocked out cold from sitting up suddenly when his fly was unexpectedly unzipped.

In common with the previous legend (both of them popular as newspaper fillers and anecdotes), this one has been around the country and even the world for many years, possibly existing as long as zippers have been used on men's pants flies. Sometimes the unzipped legends are combined with other accident stories, and these may conclude with the laughing-paramedics motif.

"The Videotaped Theft"

Going back at least to 1982 is the legend about a father of the bride at a society wedding who discovers that the large amount of cash he had brought in his pocket to pay the band and the caterers at his daughter's wedding reception has disappeared. He borrows money or uses a check or credit card to pay the tab. Later, while viewing a videotape of the reception taken by a camcorder left running on a tripod, he spots the bridegroom (or groom's father) taking the money from the pocket of his jacket left hanging over a chair. The thief is confronted with the tape, confesses, returns the money, and the groom agrees to an annulment, thus illustrating poetic justice (or "just deserts").

Variations of "The Videotaped Theft" have been published in newspaper and magazine articles that variously describe the event as a Catholic, Jewish, Polish, Italian, or another group's wedding and that specify different amounts of money stolen and different ways that the incident was resolved. In a letter to the "Dear Abby" advice column published in 1991 an

157

anonymous writer, who claimed to be a professional photographer, insisted that he himself had videotaped the incident; he asked Abby how to handle the situation. She advised him simply to call on the bride's father and show him the tape without offering any explanation whatever.

Significantly, although this legend was very popular through the 1980s and 1990s, nobody, not even some priests and ministers who tell the story, has yet produced a copy of the actual tape.

"The War Profiteer"

During World War II a pair of women were overheard talking on a bus or subway about how well their husbands were doing as manufacturers of arms or other war supplies. "I wish the war would go on forever," one of them commented. Another passenger came over and slapped the speaker, saying, "That's for my son who is fighting [or was killed] in the South Pacific [or Europe]. Sometimes there were two slaps, one for each of two military sons.

Although reported in *Time* magazine in 1942 and repeated during the war years with several variations, the incident was never verified by a witness or participant. Other similar stories described various rebukes to people who spoke in favor of the war or against America's fighting troops or who mocked a disabled young person, not realizing that he or she had been wounded or maimed by enemy action.

"Which Tire?"

This typical tricky-question story from academe illustrates how an instructor may foil students' attempts to pass an examination that they had failed to attend at the scheduled time. Two students from the same class party the night before the exam and sleep through the alarm clock. They offer the excuse that they were out of town and had a flat tire coming back to campus that prevented them from arriving on time. Their professor agrees to give them makeup exams but puts the students in separate rooms. The first question on the test is "Which tire?"

Several versions of this story name an actual professor at a specific university, and this individual may, indeed, have used the ploy, or at least claimed to have used it. But the story of the "Which tire?" exam is widespread and long-lived as well as resembling other tricky Q-and-A legends such as "Define 'Courage'" and "The One-Word Exam Question."

"The Wrong Car"

The above title gives away the plot of this recent legend, which might better be called "Sticking Up for One's Rights." The story that circulated on the Internet starting in 1998 was that an elderly woman was advised by her son to carry a small handgun in her purse for protection. She complied and soon had occasion to pull the weapon on someone, since she returned to her car in the mall's parking lot to find two men sitting in it, drinking beer, and eating. Brandishing the gun, the woman ordered the men from the car, and they quickly ran away. But her key did not fit the ignition, and the woman soon noticed her own look-alike car parked nearby.

Some versions of the story end with the woman going to the mall's security office to report that she tried to start the wrong car. Before she can fully explain, however, the security officer tells her that he doesn't have time for her report since there's a crazy woman running around the lot with a gun, ordering people out of their cars. Several versions of the story also included a racist element, with the woman being white and the men ordered from their car being black or Hispanic.

"The Wrong Rest Stop"

An automobile legend known in Australia (and perhaps elsewhere) concerns the "escape lanes" (safety ramps) provided for heavy trucks on hilly major highways. The Australian versions are set in specific locations, such as the "Devil's Elbow" hairpin bends in the hills above Adelaide. On one such dangerous grade, a truck driver realizes that he has lost his brakes and struggles to keep the big rig upright as he roars around the tight turns of the steep road, praying he will be able to make it to the escape lane. Just as he rounds the last bend before the ramp—still holding the truck on the road—he sees to his horror a family halfway up the ramp having a picnic.

The Ultimate Urban Legends

The Ultimate Urban Legends

2007 PINKMINT PUBLICATIONS.